W9-AAD-747

Advance Praise for *Into the Heat*

Meet Cindy Bellinger, the self-reliant heroine of this true tale about living on the edge of the wilderness in the company of a woodstove and a vivid cast of male characters. Bellinger's writing is as clear and crisp as a winter morning, and her unflinching assessment of her dual loves of relationship and the solitary life of a writer...will make you sit up and ask yourself: What have I been doing with *my* life?

Lisa Dale Norton, Shimmering Images: A Handy Little Guide to Writing Memoir

Cindy captures the art, spirituality and hard work of wood gathering and its relation to the flow of her life. Her descriptions of trees, men, dogs, her woodstove...portray her love of nature and an alternative lifestyle.

Dixie Boyle, Between Land & Sky: A Fire Lookout Story

Into the Heat

Books by the Author

Wild Honey (Young Adult novel, ebook)

Journaling for Women: *Write, Doodle, Scribble! and Meet Yourself Up Close*

Waterwise Garden Care: *Your Practical Guide*

Someone Stole My Outhouse: *And Other Tales of Home Improvement*

Into the Heat

My Love Affair
with
Trees, Fire, Saws & Men

Cindy Bellinger

**BLUE MESA
BOOKS**

Santa Fe, New Mexico

Into the Heat, My Love Affair with Trees, Fire, Saws & Men
By Cindy Bellinger

Copyright ©2011 Cindy Bellinger

Blue Mesa Books, LLC
304 Calle Oso
Santa Fe, NM 87501
www.bluemesabooks.com

The artwork on the cover is "Early Winter," a
24 x 30-inch pastel by Elizabeth Sandia.

ISBN: 978-0-9839435-2-5
LCCN: 2011922664

Printed in the United States

For my father,
who let me strike matches
when I was just itty-bitty.

CONTENTS

Windfall

❧

A TREE FELL. NOTHING SIMPLER THAN that. I rounded a bend and there it was. A tree. A whole tree stretched across the trail. Seeing it down took my breath away. I stood and stared. I knew this tree. A sturdy ponderosa with no outward sign of disease, it shouldn't have toppled over. At one hundred feet tall—or long, now—it was big, its demise hard to take in. My dogs paced and sniffed. We often stopped here for a quick rest before heading home after a long hike. Now they looked up at me, whining and wanting some reassurance that everything was okay. It wasn't easy to give them that.

Things change rapidly in a forest. For periods of time, all feels stable then suddenly it's not. You have to be brave living here. If maintaining the status quo is important, it's not wise to live beneath pines. They split. They break. Nothing remains the same; even the strongest trees with the widest girths can't be counted on forever. Trees teach impermanence; this much I've learned—and keep relearning, especially after every high wind.

In 1997 I bought a place in the middle of a forest in northern New Mexico. Ever after I'd refer to the house as a rundown shack, yet it quickly became home. In a small enclave of seven houses my place is less than a third of an acre, "just a measly lot," someone said contemptuously. But when your backyard touches thousands of wilderness acres, who needs to own more? Thoroughly delighted that a whole mountainside rose behind my new home, I began exploring even before I had the furniture arranged. The area hadn't burned in ages, hadn't been logged in a century, if ever. Dense and tangled, the forest resembled a huge, overgrown hedge. There was no easy entrance; so one branch at a time I began carving a labyrinth of trails that today has become my lifeline. For many reasons, mostly to keep peace in myself, I go daily into the forest.

When I first began poking around in the woods, it didn't take much to realize my good fortune. Right before my eyes was a never-ending supply of kindling. For years my only source of heat has been wood so when coming upon this immeasurable wealth of twigs, I danced a little jig. I love an abundance of downed branches. After all, I'm a wood gatherer, and have been even before I can remember.

"You'd just turned two the first time we went camping," my mother told me once. "When we were setting up the tent, you toddled off by yourself and came back carrying a pine cone. You put it down by the grill, right where it belonged, just like you knew what you were doing."

But I did know what I was doing. From that primal time when we first found fire, when we first discovered the heat and comfort of fire, and when our strands of DNA were first encoded, mine said: gather wood.

This book is about living with a woodstove and gathering all the wood needed to feed it. Bringing home the downed tree is just a part. I share my fondness for rural living that began when I was a kid watching my father build fires in our fireplace. He dealt with wood throughout each season, creating a rhythm of activity that became a touchstone for me. What I learned from watching my mother weaves another kind of story. Disgruntled with my father, she yearned for a life that was a little wilder. However this works, I ended up living the life she wanted. This meant joining that long winding road some women travel going from man to man. Never settle for less is the message I got, meaning there might be something better just around the bend. So basically, I never settled at all, or at least not for long. Until moving to the forest.

The benefit of living alone and heating with wood is giving myself over to flames like to a lover. On cold, snowy nights I can easily fall into a trance of sensuality before a fire and stay that way for hours reflecting, thinking, feeling safe and secure. Making sense out of life's many phases never unfolds sequentially, and my story weaves odd moments from the past that tuck right in with the present, many of the connections gleaned from sitting in front of a fire.

Finding the big ponderosa down was a delight. This was a lot of wood, an incredible amount of good luck. I also knew hauling this log out of the forest would not be easy, though not impossible. By then I'd fashioned a lifestyle devoted to finding wood and came to love trees for providing it.

This is how I've always wanted to live: close enough to touch the earth's skin. Yet it took a twelve-year-old girl to unknowingly set me on the way.

One

If I reach back far enough, the genesis for this story begins the night I met Ted during a Colorado snowstorm in 1978. We both had landed in a truck-stop café in the middle of nowhere. I was waiting for the child in my charge to return by bus from Santa Fe where she'd been visiting her father. Ted was returning to New Mexico after visiting his parents in Denver. We talked, traded phone numbers, began a long distant courtship and the following spring after getting my teaching certificate, I moved to Los Alamos to live with and eventually marry Ted. Slowly I inched my way into journalism with all thoughts of being a teacher falling by the wayside. Seven years later after we divorced, I sent a barrage of letters to school districts around the state. It was time to take up where I'd left off, and I entered a ten-year stint of teaching junior high English and reading. How I loved the kids! I didn't love the school system and had little regret as I wormed my way back into journalism.

Yet every year when that first tinge of fall begins and school buses begin rolling again, I long for the classroom. The spring of 1994 marked my seventh year of teaching, my second year of working in a Catholic school in Santa Fe. One morning a small, thin girl with stringy dark hair stayed after class. A seventh grader, Lisa rarely spoke so for her to linger with something to say was most unusual.

"Miss B, you know how I imagine you?" she said shyly, holding an armload of books in front of her mouth, making herself nearly inaudible.

"Go ahead, tell me." I often marveled how often kids blurted out something that invariably held the answer to a private question or provided some scrap of needed information. Junior high kids possess an uncanny intuition that lets them name the unnamable. And they nail it every time.

Lisa took a deep breath. "I always imagine you sitting in front of a fire with lots of pillows. You have cats in your lap and there are piles of books all around you," she mumbled.

Stunned, I stared at this little wisp of a prophet who had described exactly what was missing in my life. I lived in Santa Fe in a studio apartment with radiant floor heating, no cats, no fluffy pillows, and hardly any time to read. For the rest of the day I held the image Lisa had given me like a jewel, a vision I could sink into.

Soon after, as if she had gently kicked a cog in motion, things began turning.

As the semester wound down, word came that I'd gotten a grant from the National Endowment for Humanities to study fairy tales that summer at Wayne State University in Detroit. The eleven other participants and I boarded in an off-campus apartment building aptly named The Forest, a perfect place to live while studying witches, castles, and princes wandering around looking for pretty girls to kiss. One afternoon a group of us headed downtown, and deep in an older section of town we discovered a department store of a bygone era with thick wooden doors and richly varnished shelves. There on a rack was the most wonderful coat. Lightweight and roomy, it was perfect for chopping kindling.

Many years had passed since Ted and I had lived in the mountains, heating our house with a woodstove. I'd secretly longed for that lifestyle again.

"Just look at this coat. It's perfect for chopping wood," I exclaimed.

"Do you chop wood?" one of the women asked.

"Well, not anymore, but…"

They rolled their eyes; yet that khaki coat with snaps down the front was one of those finds you can't pass up. Besides, as I carried the bag out the door, the feeling persisted that this was meant to be.

Not long after I returned from Detroit, the man I'd been dating for three years took me out to dinner. Fulton was vivacious and believed all the possibilities for life were at his fingertips. His speed was full-tilt and nothing less. He wined and dined me and was always inventing fun get-aways. He rented an apartment in town but owned a tiny place along the Pecos River, thirty miles to the east. When we first started dating, he asked me to come to his place in the country for the weekend. Upon arriving, the first thing I noticed was a spectacular cliff along the other side of the river. I immediately fell in love with that cliff and began looking forward to spending weekends there.

The Pecos River is what people call a stream in other parts of the country. Only twenty feet wide in some places it's easy to ford during the drier seasons. On my first visit after we walked down to the water then returned to the house, Fulton asked if he could freshen my drink. And out of the blue, a flash—one of those gut-wrenching, other-worldly knowings—shrieked inside me that it didn't matter which woman was with him, only that one was. I admonished myself to stop imagining things. I turned my head and fell into a very rocky relationship.

Glad to see me after my month away in Detroit, Fulton took me to a fancy restaurant and began the evening by suggesting the most wondrous thing: That I put a trailer on the back of his property. Perfect. At one point we'd tried living together, a most disastrous experiment. If we could live close to each other that just might work. Both hands in my lap hidden by the crisp white tablecloth, I pinched myself. I knew that Detroit coat hanging in my closet was magic, and silently I thanked a stranger I'd met at a yard sale several years before. Her story helped me trust the power of life's intricate ways.

Both of us rummaging through kitchen utensils, we got to chatting. She was a retired chef and began reminiscing about her life's one grand adventure. "It all began in a way I never would have dreamed," she said. "I'd been wanting a change. Then traveling up the California coast, I stopped at a shop that had a sign out front: 'We buy junk and sell antiques.' I found a small model of an old whaling ship. Boats had never interested me, but for some reason I had to have that ship."

For a year it sat on her living room shelf. Then someone she knew, knew someone who was looking for a cook aboard a yacht to sail around the world. "Oddly enough, seeing that ship everyday prepared me for something I never would have considered." The job lasted five years.

So my Detroit coat had became my ship, my talisman, quietly hanging in my closet and gathering all the threads needed to bring about my dream—coming to know a piece of land by heart. In time, living that dream began resembling black magic, but who are we to say what isn't necessary?

Two

This morning the coyotes woke me long before dawn, and I guessed they were coming for the apple cores. My neighbor Sloan and I had picked apples the day before from a wild scraggily tree near an old homestead. Several years have passed since I finagled him to help bring the downed tree home; it was the main event that finally brought us together. After making an apple pie from our meager harvest, I took the scraps over to Sloan. He likes leaving pieces of fruit for forest visitors.

"Those coyotes aren't afraid one bit to come by for a snack," Sloan said once. He keeps a battered pair of binoculars near his chair for up-close views of all the goings-on in his yard—birds, chipmunks, squirrels. And one time a bear. He's even named a few of the regular rabbits. Periodically, he spots a fox slinking around looking for tidbits. Only once during the day has a coyote trotted by in that low-slung way of theirs; they usually sneak in at night to steal the apples. This morning after hearing the coyotes, I got up, put tea water on to boil, built a fire, and listened. They had to be right there, right in Sloan's backyard.

Sloan himself is a feral looking man with long silver hair that he ties back in a ponytail. His thick white beard gets bushy between trimmings. In country parlance, he lives "across the way." Not even down the road a tad. With all the trees surrounding his place, though, you wouldn't even know it's there. He continues transplanting cedar seedlings along the front perimeter. He likes to keep things hidden, including much of his inner self.

On my first official day here, after my phase along the river ended, I went around and introduced myself to the fulltime neighbors, only two then. The other houses were summer homes. A family with two kids lived directly next door. "If you ever need any help, just let us know," the man said. I thanked him and moved on, but trying to even find the door to the second house was tricky. I made my way behind a hedge of cedars and carefully climbed the rotting wooden stairs to a sagging porch. I knocked on the screen door. A big muscular man cautiously stepped from the house. We chatted for maybe a minute before he ducked inside again.

Over many years Sloan and I finally moved beyond neighbors into friends then into something more, and we like talking about our first impressions that day. We both thought: Hmmm, not bad. Going between our houses takes maybe thirty seconds, "forty steps out" he said one day. Now some mornings I slip from his house and scurry home in my robe and slippers. Life holds so many circular events. You just never know how things will turn out.

When I first moved here to the forest, the sounds of the coyotes on the ridge behind the houses became a kind of anchor. It was June and nearly every evening I found myself listening for their ruckus. I hadn't known something so wild could fasten me so quickly to a place. Depending on the season, the coyotes congregate in certain spots on the mountainside, often calling in recruits for their evening refrains. Off to the north one starts and another answers from the east. Pretty soon the forest fills with yaps and high pitched yelps. Because of this, I know where home is.

No dogs accompanied me on my first ramblings here. They came five years later. First Lady, then Emma. In their own animalness they've also settled me into routine. Each morning I open the door seemingly to let them out, but I too step onto the porch. Especially in winter, that initial blast of chill is like diving into a cold mountain lake, most welcome after snuggling under a pile of warm blankets all night. Every morning—no matter what—my young dog, Emma, looks expectantly at my green canvas satchel, the one I use for gathering kindling and keep on a hook by the door. She knows when I take it down, a walk is in order.

Early one summer morning I eagerly put on my hiking clothes after letting the dogs out. All night a big off-season wind had ripped through the area. The forest floor would be strewn with downed branches. Much to the dogs' delight, I grabbed the carrying bag, my walking stick, and set out. We headed up Slow and Easy, a trail that follows the high side of a small *arroyo* or gully. Twenty minutes into the walk we came upon the toppled ponderosa. I stopped dead in my tracks, as if caught by a spell.

Newly downed trees are a frequent sight here and most don't surprise me. Through the seasons the weaker trees slowly wither from a variety of mishaps. I've watched perfectly fine trees get squeezed out by others that had a slightly better spot of sunlight. Years ago a drought prompted an infestation of the Ips bark beetle on piñon trees. Only those growing in depressions and along waterways were immune. Lightning also kills trees. Sometimes when struck the bark explodes off a tree, and that's it. Finished. Sometimes a blast will slice a trunk right down the middle, top to bottom. Less violent strikes can still be pervasive. A small stand of six ponderosas died from lightning after the tallest got hit, their roots were so entwined.

I stared at this newly downed ponderosa, disbelieving. I'd come to know this tree. Never once had I imagined it would go. I wasn't the only one drawn to it. Steller's jays frequented its branches. I also got my first glimpse of peewees in this tree as the tiny birds paused in their northern migration. Safe behind clusters of pine needles a squirrel sometimes scolded as the dogs and I passed.

For many of us forest creatures this tree was a solid pillar, dependable. Before it fell, a jumble of rocks protruded near its trunk, and one stuck out like a shelf. After a long afternoon of hiking, I welcomed this seat under a canopy of deep shade and always stopped here to give the dogs a lap of water before heading home. Now with the tree down, the rocks had shifted and my sitting place was no longer.

I'm not sure when I first began calling this tree Papa South; the name came one day and stuck. A few trees along my paths have become like family, so naming certain ones seemed natural. For awhile I was pen pals with author Bernd Heinrich, a biology professor at the University of Vermont whose specialty is ravens and forest management. After reading his book *Ravens in Winter*, I wrote him about raven antics I'd seen in nearby fields, and we ended up exchanging notes for well over a year. Later he wrote *The Trees in My Forest* and said knowing one tree is like recognizing a good friend. Recently I read that a native tribe in New Zealand keeps names for the tallest and oldest trees, a form of affection and reverence.

Though some trees might feel female and others male, ponderosas are *monoecious*, a mix of Greek and Latin that means "one house." That is, a plant with both male and female parts that simultaneously pollinate and form seeds. This particular ponderosa that I'd become friends with stood south of the trail, and for whatever reason seemed like a kindly old grandfather. So Papa South it was.

And now he was down.

More than a little dismayed I took a deep breath and walked on. Usually there's a feeling of symbiotic union with the forest as I gather twigs and branches. This time I picked up bits of windfall unceremoniously and by the dogs' standards headed home way too soon.

Three

I made a vow last summer to be up and ready each morning to watch the sunrise. My picture window looks out to a layered cliff cut millions of years ago by the river. Shelves of sandstone travel lengthwise, curving into a small amphitheater that has no echo. Each day the show begins when sunlight touches the canyon rim, a ragged contour of treetops against the sky. Then slowly like a tracking beam, light draws the canyon wall out of shadow, and the sun-drenched details of shallow caves pock the face of the cliff.

This is the same cliff along the same river across from Fulton's land, only now I'm many miles upstream and many years down the road. When Fulton suggested bringing in a mobile home, I had no idea this was the third time he'd proposed such a thing. The first woman had a camper on the back of a truck near his house. The second woman pulled a small travel trailer into the orchard. How interesting that in the swirl of connectedness that living tends to create, I later met one woman who knew the other.

Unsuspecting of being part of a pattern, I eagerly placed an order for a new doublewide. And oh! the dreams I had. Big ones. I envisioned grazing sheep and outlined a place for a small barn. I sketched a prolific garden and even mapped out a root cellar. This would be the patch of land I'd learn by heart. I planned and dreamed, and each day went to work in a high state of excitement.

Lisa, my little wisp of a prophet, was now in the eighth grade. I saw her frequently in the halls. She'd changed over the summer as seventh graders are wont to do; they lose a shade of innocence. Yet in the sass of the eighth graders roaming the halls, I was pleased to see Lisa blooming. She'd been accepted into a crowd of academically inclined kids and even ran for class secretary. We'd pass in the hallway and smile. We never spoke again but the words she'd said to me had been perfect, and enough.

From order to delivery, it took three months for the doublewide to arrive. During that time, Fulton and I lived in his small house along the river, somehow working gracefully around our differences; those three months turned out to be our best. One fall day in particular still stands out—the first day I wore my new Detroit coat.

Fulton heated his place with a woodstove and had gotten a delivery of wood. Some of the pieces were too long. Wanting some exercise, I volunteered to cut the wood. I'd also picked apples in the orchard where my doublewide would sit. I wanted to make a pie and was in a quandary.

"There's a game on TV that I want to watch," offered Fulton, always one to cut a deal. "I'll peel the apples if you saw the wood." Now, most women wouldn't see this as much of a bargain. But the hardest part of making an apple pie is peeling the apples. Then again, I hadn't handled a chainsaw in a long time. It'd been nine years since I'd been married to Ted, a small man who loved big tools. I'd taken to using tools as a kid; Ted helped refine my skills, and we worked well together on projects around the yard and house. He took photos one day while I shoveled gravel, sand, and cement into a mixer. I've never shied away from heavy physical work. But I do have my limits, especially when it came to Ted's gas chainsaw. Heavy, hard to hold, and hard to start, it scared me. But Fulton was a man who liked the easy life. He had an electric chainsaw. He plugged in a long extension cord, showed me the on/off switch, and away I went.

And there we were: The man in the house peeling apples and the woman outside sawing logs.

A chainsaw is a quick teacher. The first lesson is wood likes to drop off freely and cleanly. If it can't, more than likely the chain will jam up. Do that a few times and you'll figure things out. I soon rigged up a primitive stand by rolling two logs together; in the crotch between them I laid a third piece of wood, the longer one that needed cutting. The arrangement let me fall into a routine: position wood, start the saw, touch the blade to the log, and find a way in.

Wood needs to be ridden. Some is smooth going; other pieces jerk you around making it hard to hold the saw. What you're doing is traversing the grain and there's no way to know how a slice will go until you're in it. You're cutting through growth rings. Only for a moment did I let myself realize this wood was once alive. Chainsaws don't let you ponder that sort of thing. There are more crucial things to consider: Which way is the blade facing? Where are your hands? Is everything out of the way? Once you're ready, the teacher whirrs away, and you better not even consider daydreaming.

A pile of wood began adding up and the high pitched whine of my saw joined others up and down the river. The day initiated me into that long tradition of cutting wood for winter. Best of all, my Detroit coat turned out just as I'd imagined; it was perfect. And still is. For eighteen years now I've worn that soft khaki coat while gathering branches or chopping kindling during blizzards. One winter day after thrashing my way into a stand of scrub oak to collect dead stalks for kindling, a patch of sunlight lured me beneath a ponderosa. The day was warm, thirty degrees, a winter heat wave. I took off my coat, spread it over a bed of pine needles, and Emma in her puppy way sidled up next to me. She put her paws on my arm and we took a forest snooze.

If I get too warm hiking or picking up branches, I often leave my coat hanging from branches, thrown over scrub oak or folded on a rock. Sometimes I forget and have to go back the next day. No one frequents this neck of the woods except me and my dogs or my part-time neighbors, Rodger and Julie and their dogs.

"Saw your coat the other day," Rodger said once. "I figured you'd be back for it."

I toss my coat over a bush the way I do over a chair in the living room. This is where I live.

The day after finding Papa South down, I excitedly packed up a pair of leather work gloves and a folding saw, a trusty tool that fits perfectly in my fanny pack. The area behind my house is checkered with private and public land. When first moving here, I'd been quick to get permission to tramp around on the various private properties and since the tree fell on the Baca's land, I felt no qualms about cutting it to make a detour. It had toppled across the trail and in my mind was now in the way. First, though, I needed to sit on the thick trunk and experience this tree differently. Then I began walking beside it, high-stepping over the branches; the immensity awed me. A live tree swaying in the slightest breeze holds power. A downed tree is a finite thing. Done. The incongruity was unsettling.

One seldom gets a chance to walk in the crown, the uppermost branches of a tree, and in an odd inverse of perspective I was on the top and bottom at the same time. With this in mind, walking among the branches made me a little dizzy. Still, I spent some time admiring the view. It was mid-June; all the trees had finished candling, putting out that year's new growth. The term "candling" is well put, especially when it comes to firs and spruces. Their iridescent yellow-green tips look exactly like little lit candles. No wonder the tradition of stringing lights on Christmas trees is so ingrained: Candling, whether with electric lights or new spring needles, holds all the anticipation of longer days with more sun. On fir trees the velvety soft, newly candled tips even feel cool, nothing like the bristly new growth of ponderosas.

I bent over and ran my fingers through the needles. When ponderosas candle, at the end of every branch a thick cluster forms, new growth encased in a scaly conical nubbin. These always look like the beginnings of tiny cones, only on closer inspection they are packets of itty-bitty not-yet-born needles. Sometimes protrusions develop on either side. Some turn into the seed-bearing female pine cones; others grow into the elongated, scaly male appendages that in a few months bulge with pollen.

The first few years living here I eyed the candling process closely and watched the tips of the tallest trees reach up a little more each summer. Much later I learned about a specialized field of research that studies the crowns or canopies of trees.

In 1969 Bill Dennison, a young biologist stationed at the H.J. Andrews Experimental Forest, suspected tree canopies held answers to many diverse questions. The site, comprised of 16,000 acres in west-central Oregon, was set aside in 1948 by the Forest Service to do research on old growth trees. Dennison insisted there was much more to old growth forests than big trees and spearheaded an unprecedented experiment. He recruited two women who were experienced rock climbers. They strapped on cliff-climbing gear and traveled into a tree. That ascent opened a frontier science. Today large cranes swing baskets over the tops of forests as scientists gather data on everything from the vertical habitats of song birds to the chemical alterations of rainwater before it touches the ground.

As I continued stepping over the limbs, I wondered: Shouldn't there be more noise after a tree goes down? Some reverberation? Some gasping? Then, of course, that proverbial question arises: If someone isn't around to hear a tree fall, does it make any noise? We always assume this "someone" is human. Surely a rabbit holed up in a nearby bush heeded the whoosh as the tree gave way. No doubt birds all tucked in for the night woke and sprang for safer perches.

After one last look at my downed tree, I stepped forward, unfolded the saw and began cutting branches for the detour. My musings continued: Were they trembling? Were these branches shocked at the sudden collapse of their world? Plunging to earth would certainly cause pain; and trauma irreversibly changes lives no matter what. When everything we believe turns upside down, cells freeze. Nothing moves. Maybe that's why the needles on Papa South took so long to brown. Maybe they just couldn't believe it.

Four

When Sloan and I first began hiking together, I quickened to realize how observant he was. He could track the passings of animals in the summer. Gnawed bark, he said, was from porcupines. He could tell because of the teeth marks. Tufts of needles below ponderosas meant squirrel foraging in the fall. The tassel-earred, sometimes called the Abert's squirrel, is symbiotic with ponderosas. Solely dependent on these trees for food and shelter, the squirrels in turn eat a fungus that grows nearby; their excrement then permeates the soil and the nutrients are taken up by the ponderosa roots. These squirrels are only found in ponderosa forests in the Southwest. I fell into learning from Sloan. But he also learned a few things from me.

At one point he was reading *Clan of the Cave Bear* by Jean M. Auel, a novel set in Neanderthal times, and was curious about the moss those early people used for their prehistoric candles. I knew just where to find it. One tree hosted so much moss the bark was green and hairy. I led the way and Sloan gathered a small sack, and he fashioned a rustic lantern by pouring oil deep into a recession in a rock he'd found. We used that primitive lantern all summer sitting on his porch in the evenings. The experience became a balm, letting me know a new path was under my feet. The sensitivity that this man showed in relation to the natural world opened my own eyes to ever smaller details going on in the forest.

Fulton hadn't been an astute observer of things nearby, and I tried believing this didn't matter. But one morning he sat on the deck reading in the warm autumn sun. I headed to the river to see what I could see. As a kid I loved poking around tide pools at the beach only a few blocks from our home. Both my parents were sharp when it came to the natural world. At the beach they taught me to identify many shells and fish, even kelp. On day trips into Lucerne Valley where relatives leased acres of cropland, we'd stop along a freshwater stream on the way home. My mother showed me and my little sister Cathy how to find watercress. We ate handfuls plucked from the sandy banks then gathered enough for salad that night at home. Along the muddy edges of the Pecos River I discovered caddis fly casings and skippers. Minnows darted among rocks and submerged roots. A teeming tiny world was always underway.

When I went to the river that day, the water was low and in some spots I could cross to the other side, hopping along a series of dry flat boulders. I found a few rocks smoothly rounded from tumbling in the river and tucked them in my pocket. Then I found a wondrous stone.

"What a find," I exclaimed outloud and scurried back up the hill, burning with excitement. What a treasure. In my palm rested a small black oval rock only an inch long. Thin white veins engulfed the stone, etching it with tracings like some ancient subliminal language. Flattened on one end, it stood solidly by itself like a tiny monument. I set it on the porch railing. "Isn't it just incredible?" I gushed.

Fulton picked it up, looked for two seconds, and his forehead furrowed. He shrugged and handed it back.

We weren't curious about each other's world. I can see that now. Our differences could have opened luscious possibilities, but only if we had wondered about the finer points of the other. With my stone discredited, I felt slighted. When I couldn't converse about business, did Fulton feel devalued? When it came to his work, he was farsighted. My vision was at ground level, burrowing in. We traveled such different dimensions that we slipped right by one another. Yet we continued on. Denial has thrown sand in lovers' eyes for as long as rivers have been tumbling hieroglyphics onto stones.

As I sawed away at Papa South, the scent of terpenes or tree oils, levitated by the sun, brought thoughts of my father. I was five years old when Daddy began painting boats down on the docks in Newport Beach in southern California. He held that job until I was out of high school, until boats were made of fiberglass and no longer required anyone who knew how to sand, stain, and varnish wood. For as long as I can remember Daddy came home each evening smelling of turpentine. Even today the slightest whiff of paint thinner ignites memories of my father. If my little sister Cathy and I stepped on tar on the beach, before letting us in the house Daddy would open a can of turpentine, wet an old rag, and clean us up. Now as my fingers got sticky from the pine resin, I pinched small handfuls of dirt to quell the stickiness until I got back home and could clean up once more with turpentine.

The sap ran thick. Sometimes green wood doesn't yield easily and now with the pitch oozing freely, the job became messy; but I soon fell into a rhythm of sawing and tossing branches into a pile. I remembered *The Giving Tree* by Shel Silverstein, a children's book with adult wisdom. A tree loves the little boy who climbs its branches; it loves the same boy, now a young man, when he cuts the tree to make a house. In the end the tree feels honored when the same boy, now an old man, needs to rest on the tree's stump. Relationships are as fluid as water, bumping into obstacles, moving around them, through them, over them. Papa South and I had certainly changed course. Rather than being two alive and thriving entities, one of us had entered a new category. This tree was now firewood. Pure and simple.

I knew taking this tree out of the forest would not be a one woman job. Alone I could clear the detour, though even that would be no small task. Hauling the entire tree out would push the boundaries of the word "chore." Harvesting large diameter trees takes machinery.

Some big decisions and long days lay ahead. Only one thing was sure. Dry wood is easier to cut and lighter to carry than green. I prefer aging stove wood two years so leaving Papa South to season right there in the forest made the most sense. There was no rush.

Done with the day's work I folded up my saw and headed higher into the mountains, much to Lady and Emma's immediate approval. Leaving the downed tree I envisioned burning Papa South as a form of worship. I love fires made from wood that I know. What I couldn't possibly have guessed then was the deep apology I'd bring to that first fire made with Papa South.

Five

The day I whittled the wood down to fit Fulton's woodstove was probably the last good day between us. We laughed the rest of the evening over our division of labor and sat before a chirpy fire eating fresh apple pie. Autumn in northern New Mexico doesn't get any better than this. But the days ahead were darkening and not only from the fading winter light.

I'd had a permanent foundation poured on the back of Fulton's land, and my doublewide arrived a few days before New Years. Quickly a crew put it together and hooked up the utilities. Fulton helped carry boxes and arrange the furniture. With long strides the time between our two houses clocked in at forty-nine seconds, the perfect distance for living together separately. A few weeks after I'd moved in, we walked a road that ran atop the cliff above the river. In photos we took that day a definitive footpath already curved between our two places. In the beginning we traveled the distance often and casually—

dinners at his place or mine, sleepovers either way; we came and went like we had two homes.

The best part for me was having a woodstove again, a real one, one that worked. After divorcing Ted, I had lived with a woman named Sarah in the hills behind Santa Fe. The house did have something that resembled a woodstove. But it leaked heat and every crack seeped smoke. The thing was so tiny you practically had to crawl on top of it to feel any warmth at all. So having an efficient woodstove fitted with a glass door to see the flames made me dance that little jig again.

When Ted and I first began living together, friends said cutting our own wood was the way to go. "You'll get a supply laid in for winter and won't have to pay for it," they said. So I got a woodcutting permit from the Forest Service. Ted bought an old truck and a new chainsaw. Early one Saturday morning I made lunch, and we set out. And never went again. The day was grueling. Besides, all that "free" wood ended up costing $1,700. Then we had to rent a wood splitter. Then the wood needed to season before we could burn it. All this meant that before winter hit we needed to get a cord of wood that was split and dry and ready to burn. What a cord was we had no idea, but people said to get it from guys along the road. Ted said he'd get one after work.

I was in the kitchen washing dishes when he pulled up alongside the curb. A truck hauling a horse trailer loaded with wood drove in behind him. He came running down our lawn. "Hey, come look at the wood I bought," he called, bursting into the house. I dried my hands and followed him back outside. Though the wood looked good, something didn't feel right. For many years my family had had horses. I walked around the trailer, peered in, stepped off to the side. I was considering something.

"So what do you think?" Ted kept asking. He was pleased with his find.

"Let me think a minute," I said, walking around and peering into the trailer. The guys were getting antsy. Then I got it. "Horse trailers have a compartment up front for saddles and hay so the trailer isn't completely full." I looked the guys full on and they backed down on the price. I still have the photo of me standing on "my" pile of wood. Sometimes you don't need to know anything about wood. You need to know horse trailers.

By direct calculation a cord comes to 128 cubic feet, ideally measuring 4-feet high by 4-feet wide by 8-feet long. My stacks are never that noble, always too short or too high no matter what direction. But "a cord" is also used as a form of barter even with no measuring involved, especially when dealing with guys selling wood along the road. As I anticipated the delivery of wood for the doublewide, I was relieved to be free from that gamble. You never know what some shyster is trying to pull.

A friend once bought a truck load of wood from along the road and when the guy delivered it, he'd switched loads on her. "He had a trailer full of little limbs, not the split wood I'd bought," she reported. Another story has it that a highway vendor asked for half the payment before delivery. He never showed up with the wood.

After I began living with Sarah and that wretched little woodstove, I came home after work one evening and noticed a huge pile of wood out front. Sarah came dashing out of the house. "Look! I got a great deal on some wood," she beamed. "I got it alongside the road. The guys were real nice."

I stopped and looked at it. The pulp was soft and crumbling apart in chunks. At some point wood begins the process of becoming paper. "I hope you didn't pay much. It's rotten."

The smile on her face fell. And all that winter nothing but rotten heat came out of that miserable little stove. This is exactly what the guys along the road hope for: Some dumb broad coming along willing to pay good money for bad wood. Sarah isn't dumb; she just didn't know wood. After many years of living here, I can now say this: When first moving to northern New Mexico, buying wood alongside the road is an initiation, and a way to siphon off a little innocence. Using wood for heat is rife with rituals and even before that first load of cordwood arrived at the doublewide, I had two galvanized metal buckets at the ready. When I'd first begun living with Ted and making fires, the ashes piled up quickly. One morning I went to the local hardware store for a fireplace shovel. Back home, I grabbed a pink plastic bucket from the yard and commenced to scooping out the ashes. I set the bucket on the carpet, thinking I'd get rid of them somehow—later. I built a fire and went about my day.

In those early days after Ted left for work, I spent each morning picking up socks, a blouse, a bra from the living room floor, leftovers from raucous nights. Before we got a couch we snuggled on the floor in the evenings amid pillows, letting our fingers unzip, unbutton, slip a strap off a shoulder. Cleaning up the remains of love on the floor was my routine before settling into my writing room for the day.

As I cleaned, I kept noticing an acrid smell stenching the house. Nothing seemed to be burning but later needing a break from writing, I decided to take the bucket outside. I lifted the handle and the entire bottom came loose. In one second red glowing embers spilled onto the carpet. I frantically shoveled the ashes onto the hearth, dashed outside and emptied the metal trash can, lugged it into the house, and shoveled in the ashes. Next came removing the molten pink plastic from the carpet. I had hoped to get the whole mess cleaned up before Ted came home. Weeks later I was still snipping carpet threads with tiny embroidery scissors to remove the plastic. He was not pleased. In time the event lost its edge, though, and he took to singing, *"There's a hole in your bucket, dear Cindy, dear Cindy. There's a hole in your bucket, dear Cindy, a hole."*

Ashes are the downside of heating with wood; they quickly accumulate. They also get everywhere. Light and feathery, they fluff up, float, and settle throughout the house no matter how carefully you shovel them out of the stove. I don't remember how my father got rid of the ashes in our fireplace when I was a kid. I just never saw him do anything with them. Which is why I had no idea how to deal with them. Which is why the plastic bucket episode remains so vivid; and why, by the time wood arrived at my doublewide, I was all set.

I'd gotten the name of a local woodsman and ordered a cord of split piñon, the favored wood here. Andrew showed up on a Friday evening in a rickety old truck, the wood piled high. A stout, muscled Hispanic man about my age, he nimbly jumped from the cab. Just before we shook hands, there was that pause, hardly discernable— that hesitation when two people from different cultures meet. Ah, he's from around here, I surmised. Since moving to New Mexico, I'd learned to recognize this pause that barely registers but persists upon meeting an Indian, Hispanic, and even another Anglo, the three prevalent cultures here. There is a distinction between all of us. For the most part it makes no difference, but sometimes it does.

One time I bought metal T-posts and a roll of fencing. A young Hispanic man led me to the supplies and that the initial hesitation was not only palpable, but a jagged fissure between us. When he couldn't contain his contempt any longer, he blatantly discounted my ability to put up the fence because I was a "fucking white lady." Everyone here, no matter which race you belong to, learns to live with it one way or another—brush it off or add it to your stack of resentments. I went home and installed the fence with the help of my friend Bonnie. We laughed about being "fucking white ladies"—especially since neither of us had had sex in a long time.

As Andrew and I chatted, puffs of steam blew from our mouths. His two workers tossed the wood off the truck into a large pile. The newly split piñon spiked the air with a rich pungency. More than anything the piñon tree is the one element that bonds the three cultures of northern New Mexico. Long before radiators, forced air heating, and solar panels everyone needed wood, no matter the way of life or culture, and piñon is abundant here. There may be a slight hesitation between all of us, yet we all know the wonderful warmth of our little stubby tree.

While Andrew and I talked, I noted he lacked the local sing-song inflection that colors so much of the Spanish dialect here. He still brings my yearly supply of split cordwood and over the years I came to learn about the time he worked in Los Angeles for nearly a decade.

"I was young and just wanted to see a little bit of the world," Andrew told me once. "You think where you grow up isn't good enough and somehow you'll make more money somewhere else." Living away from all that's familiar loosens traditions, prejudices, even speech patterns. When I taught school in a small Hispanic town in the central plains of New Mexico, my friends in Santa Fe noticed my voice assuming the local intonations of that prairie town. You pick up what you're around.

At one point Andrew's six-year-old daughter climbed out of the pickup and took her Daddy's hand. The scene was sweet, there was no hurry. But I really wanted to make that first fire. Finally the truck was empty. Andrew hoisted up his daughter then hopped in the cab, telling me to come by his woodlot. "All my customers are welcome anytime to come and get free kindling," he said. "You can have all you want."

So Andrew left and there I was with wood to make a fire, though morning brought an added chore. The wood needed to be stacked, and immediately I missed the practical side of Ted. Wood doesn't pile very high in rows before pieces start rolling off the ends, taking all your work downhill. Being a mechanical engineer, Ted designed a pipe rack that kept the wood in place, even off the ground. It worked really well. But when you leave a marriage, when you're tired of taking phone calls from the women he's seeing behind your back, you do need to leave a few things behind. In time I'd come up with another way of bracing the ends. Right now my rows were a little ragged. But at least I could look forward to a warm winter.

The next day I headed over to Andrew's to see what he had to offer. Mounds of woodpiles cover his five-acre lot near the interstate in Rowe, a tiny settlement six miles away. The ground was littered with small pieces of wood. One of my reoccurring dreams is finding money on sidewalks; the more I pick up, the more there is. The woodlot was like that dream. Everywhere were scraps of piñon, strips of cedar, chunks of this and that, all good wood scrabble for starting a fire.

Dealing with wood, whether in a house or on several acres, means a never-ending untidiness. I snicker at the catalogs selling wood racks or even slippers to wear by a fire. The settings are always spotless. Anyone who really burns wood, and not just on Christmas for that once-a-year ambience, knows a house and a yard get littered with bits of wood, everywhere and forever. When I was a kid, every Thursday afternoon was house-cleaning day. My mother, ever the Girl Scout leader with her camp clean-up charts, had one hanging in the kitchen. Cathy and I took weekly turns at every chore in the house. I actually liked vacuuming in the winter. In front of the fireplace all kinds of rattily sounds clattered up the hose, a sure sign the rug was getting clean. I still like that winter sound.

So Andrew had a win-win deal. By letting people haul away all the small stuff they wanted, he could keep the debris down around his woodlot—and at the same time let all us wood-burning fools have an endless supply of kindling. I drove an old Subaru station wagon then and with many trips to Andrew's that first winter managed to keep piles of kindling dry under green canvas tarps. You can have the biggest heap of logs imaginable. The real wealth lies in having enough kindling to start a fire.

Six

The advantage of working in a Catholic school is being able to use the word "God" without being dragged before the school board. With this in mind, I started the second semester by teaching *Where the Red Fern Grows* by Wilson Rawls. I hoped to take the kids to a deeper level of comprehension, and this book abounds with symbolism. Set in the Ozarks in 1910, the story involves eleven-year-old Billy who yearns for some coonhounds so he can hunt the river bottoms. He devises a plan, saves his money, and sends away for two puppies. The description of how he trains his dogs is a literary masterpiece. That I was now living along a river made teaching this book again even more enjoyable.

Winter was mild that year and just like Billy when he finished his farm chores, I began prowling along the river after work, bringing reports back to the classroom—the pair of ducks that hadn't left for warmer climes, how cold water looks almost solid. A tandem writing activity was having the kids listen to rocks. How stupid, they said, rocks don't talk. The assignment was to sit outside with a rock for at least five minutes each day and make notes. How different was the rock was from the day before? How did their relationship with the rock change? I brought in the small black oval stone with the white etchings one day. I led the kids through many levels of observation and their resistance loosened.

Throughout *Where the Red Fern Grows*, the simplest details turn meaningful for Billy. In answering carefully worded questions, my students found God in rustling trees, the creak of a rusty lantern handle, the howl of a mountain lion. We talked about paying closer attention to the tiniest details in our own lives to see if there might be more meaning, if God might be talking to us. Seventh graders waver precariously between being children and adults; they glimpse large truths and ask big questions. And much to their dismay, there aren't always answers even to the littlest questions.

Then right on cue something happened that added even more meaning to the story. Fulton and I had talked about getting a dog and one Friday night a mournful howl came from across the river. It lasted all night. When daylight broke, I was out the door and quickly spotted a black dot wriggling among the boulders. I roused Fulton and we brought back a very tired, very hungry puppy not more than seven weeks old. In our infinite wisdom we determined it a boy and named it Luke, only to discover it was a girl. When Monday came, Fulton had meetings all day and couldn't take her to work, so I did.

I sneaked Luke into my classroom and the students covered for me. "Quick, I hear him coming," a boy said. I handed Luke to another kid who ran into my office. That year the assistant principal had started dropping by unannounced to see if we were all "on task" and when he stepped into the room that day, we instantly became the model classroom. When I asked who could figure out what the canister of baking powder symbolized for Billy, oh the hands that went up! Even kids who were usually bored, kids who never participated in discussions, kids who always had a wisecrack all waved to get called on. The assistant principal nodded with satisfaction and left. We all laughed so hard. Another student went for Luke and we continued talking about Billy and his coonhounds. There couldn't have been a better day of show and tell.

As wonderful as some moments are, teaching is not designed to nurture the soul of teachers. The pressure at work began causing health problems. Tingling began in my hands and legs, numbness was creeping into my fingers and toes. An MRI confirmed I didn't have multiple sclerosis or a brain tumor. I next found a holistic practioner who, besides soothing me with acupuncture, asked what I most wanted to do—if I wasn't teaching. Well, a young adult novel had been roaming the back roads of my mind. I'd be writing. Excited with permission to enliven myself, that night I told Fulton my plan was to spend two hours writing each day when I got back from work. I needed to feel vital and valued, to feel like I mattered. And it needed to come from inside, from doing something creative. It was March. I could block out the first draft in two months. I'd have it done by the time we left on our trip that summer. I had a goal. Excitement coursed through me.

While listening, Fulton's jaw clenched. Finally, all he wanted to know was where he would fit in.

An aside is needed here. Men have tended to be jealous of the time I devote to writing. In an early marriage that didn't last long, my husband complained all I wanted to do was write. Ted had the same complaint and found other women who gladly gave him their time. I once lived with a poet who, instead of sharing my glee at getting poems published in obscure literary magazines, seethed with resentment. Creating huge swatches of time for myself with nothing to do but write is heavenly. Even in high school I preferred staying home weekend nights alone in my room, writing. Not long ago I culled a filing cabinet and found hundreds of short stories, poems, and the beginnings of novels that I wrote as a teenager. All on notebook paper, all written by hand. Very few were class assignments.

The goal of writing is to make passages, whole books, stories, and articles seem effortless like you just whipped them out. I like comparing well-written books to Olympic figure skaters. Flawless and graceful, the performance belies the years of practice.

Only writers understand the twenty-three drafts of *The Joy Luck Club* that Amy Tan undertook before submitting it to a publisher. We nod knowingly about the seven years it took Thoreau to write *Walden*. Then there are the thirty-nine endings of *A Farewell to Arms* that Hemingway came up with. This doesn't even count the nine different endings that F. Scott Fitzgerald suggested to him. It ain't easy, this job of moving words around. It takes hours and hours at one sitting.

"Well, you'll never be famous so why bother," said one boyfriend many years ago. Wanting fame has nothing to do with writing. You're either endowed with a gene that says write else shrivel up inside, or you're not.

So when Fulton clammed up at my announcement about writing every day, it wasn't anything new. But the core of our troubles really hinged on the fact that I like being alone. Fulton wanted too much of my spare time. I maintained my distance. And somewhere along the way we took to punishing each other—withholding affection, finding fault—all in a ruse to change the other into something more to our liking. Ironically, we were first attracted to the very things that began irritating us.

In the beginning Fulton liked my independence; I was charmed by his wide social circle. Then the novelty of get-togethers with his ex, their kids, and grandkids, began to fade, along with partying with all his friends. When we first started dating, I'd just returned from teaching in that small town in the middle of nowhere. Fulton dazzled me with trips to Mexico, the Caribbean, and it was fun sowing a few pent up wild oats. But needs change.

For all this, though, when I look back on those first days by the river, I still remember how settling into the doublewide felt like a heady marriage. After all, it was to be forever, this journey of aging alongside land that would continually renew itself. To chronicle the passage I bought a large blank spiral bound book. I pasted snips of the fabric I used for curtains. I glued down the garden plans and made notations about the birds that visited the apple trees out back. The ravens that paraded around won special entries all their own. I've kept a journal since age ten; this was the first time I'd kept one separate from my daily on-going prattlings. This is how special living here felt: elevated to prime time.

I could have been more honest, though. That heady marriage was to myself and to the dreams I had, not anything Fulton and I had in mind. For me, living in the country meant being away from distractions for more alone time. I never knew what Fulton's dreams were. Oddly enough, we never discussed what we wanted this situation to be for him or for the two of us. I'll always remember another man, a writer who passed through my life much earlier. Why that experience didn't become a blueprint for marking out yet another relationship, I don't know. Steve was upfront about what he wanted: a wife, children, the white picket fence. He also needed a woman who could help make this happen, someone a little homier. One day he said to me, "I think you and I would fight over the typewriter." I've always respected his honest appraisal. We went our separate ways and remained friends.

If only Fulton and I had talked about how living together separately might work. It was such a good idea and truly was innovative. But three months after I moved into the doublewide, it all looked better on paper.

Wood Gathering

෨

*T*ODAY AS I WRITE THIS, FOR SURE THE hundredth draft in eighteen years, a thin layer of new snow covers the ground, and I'm already planning which path to take after lunch. No doubt it'll be the one that angles up to the area where the wild turkeys like to congregate. The first time I saw their three-pointed prints crisscrossing the snow like large edgings of lace, I was thrilled. During the summer it's hard to know what lives out here. Even more than bears and mountain lions, for some reason the turkeys have come to mean pure wildness to me. Yes, I'll go in search of their markings.

After years of living in the forest, a peculiar map traces through my head, one outlined with trails leading to natural springs, to the best views of the far peaks. These trails place order on the land and richly embed the topography; how to get home is thick with direction. Like a thousand-and-one overlays of the area, this map won't ever be spread on the kitchen table. It's a collage of things known and gone. Where a Western Tanager nested one year; where a perfect arrowhead appeared after a drenching rain another year. I know where snow remains until late May—under the Douglas firs on the north slope of Bear Canyon.

This map, this knowing of ground, comes from getting lost while scouting shortcuts between canyons. It comes from walking familiar trails yet never knowing what will appear. One time half an eggshell appeared beneath a tree that I pass every day, a souvenir that fits well with my collection of bird nests. After Papa South went down, the incident fell into this map. Like fixed quadrants each downed tree gets registered. They landmark the history here. Each time I set out, this ethereal diagram unfurls before me like a chart of all that's possible and all that's been.

Day after day I kept returning to cut the detour around Papa South which soon entailed hacking through a dense stand of scrub oak. Untidy and stunted, this kind of oak doesn't even come close to those big, draping live oak trees in Texas. Preferring the drier hillsides, this scruffy shrub is stiff and scratchy, and everywhere.

I came to know scrub oak in Girl Scouts. My mother loved taking all twenty of us hiking in the coastal foothills of southern California. Scrub oak, sometimes called shrub oak was always in abundance. I didn't possess a fondness for it then and cringed upon spotting it here. Five hundred species of oak disperse across the Northern Hemisphere, eighty-five of which are found in North America. Texas alone claims forty-five different species. New Mexico has sixteen and I can count at least three behind my house.

Part of the birch family, oak belongs to the species *Quercus*; their variations reveal where they live. In wet areas huge thick-trunked oaks abound. Dry areas support the scraggly varieties. Here in New Mexico the most prevalent is Gambel's Oak. Or if you prefer Latin, *Quercus gambelii*. But the common term "scrub oak" works just as well. There are so many of the smaller, scruffy oaks that it's hard to differentiate. Scrub oak is generic no matter where you are.

Needing a larger tool for the detour job, one afternoon I hauled up a double edged pruning saw. For leveling trunks of the oak it couldn't have been better. After an hour of stacking branches off to the side that I'd retrieve later for burning, I stood back and surveyed the work. Almost there. I sawed off a small dead limb on a nearby tree, leaving about three inches to function as a hook, and hung up the pruning saw. No need to lug it back and forth.

As I was about to turn something caught my eye. In one of the branches of Papa South sat a clump. I pawed my way through the needles and sure enough, a bird nest. It looked new. I cupped the nest in the palm of my hand. Some bird, heavy with eggs made this, probably sharing the task with her mate. What a feat weaving pine needles with strips of cedar. Even a piece of string was interlaced in the dense mat. No doubt she'd worked with pure optimism. And then the tree fell.

I knew about losing a home.

One

I stepped out on the porch this morning, sniffing the crisp forest air. The day is perfect for collecting kindling—not warm, not cold, and twigs are no longer covered with snow. We're in a reprieve from storms and getting out is a joy after being cooped up. Cabin fever is real: for me, for the dogs. Once I was lazy, though, and didn't go for twigs during a winter pause. A day later when we were eight inches under, I decided to venture out and break some branches. They wouldn't snap off; they bent. Had to go back for a handsaw.

With any kind of moisture—rain, snow, even low-lying clouds—the cells of trees revive. Which is why it took Papa South so long to dry, as if refusing to give up. First to go were the needles. Slowly the green slipped away, making me wonder where chlorophyll goes when it fades. Next they turned several shades of gray, from blue to pink before a rusty brown.

Even before the needles fell, the life-line of sap slowly made the limbs droop and assume a sad depressing curvature, a common shape of death.

Several years after I moved here my mother had a stroke. I flew to California and we brought her home under hospice care. I kept vigil by her death bed for several long, raw days. After each struggle with slow shallow breathing, my mother's body receded a bit more, disappearing into that private place dying people go.

I'll never forget hearing my mother's last breath. The silence was huge. Yet an odd reassurance filled the room as if the fullness of life could only be felt by witnessing the end. The privilege of being in the presence of her death buoyed me for days. Everything shimmered. The edges of tables and chairs, even people, didn't stand still. Outlines wavered, borders between here and there blurred as if being alive or dead was a veneer, no more than a matter of dimension. Months after her death, I still felt her. Though her body was gone, the woman who did watercolors at the kitchen table, the woman who rode horses every morning with a group of friends, the woman who took all us kids camping remained close by.

As I watched Papa South's brittleness arrive in increments, I was reminded how this tree also once held the vital stirrings of life. In time it would become the heart of fire. But sometimes I quickly walked by, not looking at the downed tree, just moving onward. Watching anything die is not easy.

I recently came across the engagement ring Fulton gave me. Buried in a box of trinkets, landmarks from passages long ago, the amethyst stone is the only part that still gleams. The silver band is tarnished, almost black. I took the ring off when the two of us were standing on his porch. I've often wondered what he did with the pendant I'd bought for him.

A glob of silver shaped in a female form, the pendant wasn't necessarily for him. I needed the hope that a small peaceful place in him would someday prevail, a place that was smooth and rounded, less angular. Just hold on. It'll appear. Then upon waking one morning he recounted a dream about finding a large calm lake in the middle of a clearing. Striding forward, he threw a wrench into the water. That was all he could remember, and all I needed to know.

Throwing a wrench in things was reflexive as if he needed the ensuing chaos, as if turning everything upside down was a kind of comfort zone. Take the afternoon I was on the couch reading with puppy Luke stretched out on my tummy. Fulton was leafing through a magazine at the kitchen table. Rain fell outside, a fire was going. A cozy scene. Then from out of nowhere Fulton told me he was more spiritual than I was, a typical one-upmanship in Santa Fe.

My eye still on the page, my hand still slicking down Luke's soft puppy fur, I responded: "A spiritual person wouldn't need to point that out because he is compassionate for the less evolved." The words were true, but my inner smart-ass sure sassed them out. And there we were: at it again.

I grew up watching my parents bicker. It was always something. They picked at each other relentlessly, my mother's frown lines and creases of disgust furrowing deeper and deeper through the years. I have the same creases. Finding men who know how to squabble hasn't been difficult. If they weren't adept, I taught them well. It was only after my mother's death, though, that I was able to start fitting the pieces together. My mother wanted to be an artist and live the Bohemian life. Settling down, building a house, having kids was antithesis to all her dreams. So at every chance, she snapped at my father, fraudulently blaming him for the choices she'd made. She was out to get even.

Fulton and I began seeing each other several months after my father died. I felt free from the tyranny Daddy had imposed on all our lives, and I was eager to begin anew. But patterns eerily repeat themselves. One morning Fulton made some toast; we sat at the table and I mentioned how differently we buttered it. I spread the butter; he dotted it here and there. He told me I didn't do it right and laughed, making light of it. But the moment was merely a prelude. My journals from this time overflow with his accusations: my stomach wasn't flat enough; I didn't close the shower curtain right. My best shortcoming was being too tall. His ex-wife came in under five feet. I'm five-two.

But all this was home ground. In the volleying between my parents, my father became good at belittling my mother. He whittled her down to nothing and gloated with the power of the game. My mother stayed and took it, keeping herself upright with snide, well-hurled remarks. Interestingly, Fulton adopted a gesture of ducking his head to the side whenever I spit vicious words his way.

In my twenties I had worked on a crisis hotline and learned the predictable patterns of domestic abuse. We think, surely, given enough time, the other will see the error of his or her ways. Then the fighting gets in the way of leaving. After the fighting the sex hoodwinks us into thinking all is well. I mentioned this scenario to Fulton once hoping to talk about our friction. Since he didn't hit me, he didn't see anything wrong. And for me the sex wasn't good enough to make up for the rough days. But how many women have lied? You're the *best*…that was *great*…oh, you're so *big*—superlatives all out of proportion to the reality in hand.

It gets confusing trying to pinpoint where lives start going asunder and what unravels perfectly fine relationships. Not long ago I read through my high school diaries. My preference for choosing unattainable and down-right mean, non-committing boys started when I was fourteen. My first heart-throb had a harem and I thought once he saw me, truly saw me, he'd let the others go. I went on with this theme long into adulthood because I went on finding my father every time. Not only were quarrels the norm at home but my father had affairs. Already Fulton had broken off with me to experiment with other women. Two times. I'm shamed to admit that I took him back each time. But I watched how my mother had stayed. We do what we learn even when we're old enough to know better.

More than anything, the silver pendant should have been a reminder for me and for Fulton that we were both fragile. Knowing this could have softened a lot of the corners we found ourselves in. I always hoped to muster enough love for him to transcend the ugly spots. I prayed both of us would tire of the jostling and we'd step into the daylight and breathe easier, the way you do after a scary matinee.

Both of us needed the other to be stronger. I wish we could have found a better love for each other. But we liked the fight too much.

Two

More snow started falling yesterday, and this morning it is still coming down. Lovely. But more snow means shoveling a path to the wood-pile then going back for the broom, going back to the woodpile, and sweeping off the tarps. Under one is a collection of junk wood, scraps from a friend's building project. Some of the shorter boards can be split. This entails dusting eight inches of snow off the stump that I use for a chopping block, then taking up the small ax, and going to work.

Years ago I told one of my nephews that whenever he heard about a blizzard in New Mexico, he could be sure his crazy aunt was out there splitting wood. Thirteen years old at the time and a native of southern California, he'd never seen snow and couldn't comprehend, just as my father's stories about growing up in Michigan winters fell on my own disbelieving ears.

"Sometimes it got so bad people would fasten a rope between the house and the barn so they wouldn't get lost," Daddy said.

"Why didn't they just stay inside?" I'd asked. Seemed logical to me.

"The cows need milking, the chickens need feeding. You still have chores to do when it snows," he said, adding, "even when the snow drifts get six feet high."

More than once I've been grateful the drifts here don't get that high, at least not anymore. Old timers remember the big snows. My first winter in Colorado warranted many calls to my father. He loved weather reports. When I was in the fifth grade he helped me make a two-page weekly newspaper for a few weeks. It wasn't a class project; just something I took on myself to chronicle daily temperatures, cloud formations, and wind directions. California doesn't fluctuate all that much when it comes to weather so my weekly newspaper was rather thin. To "pad it out" as he put it, Daddy encouraged me to write short anecdotes relating to the weather.

"What was it like when you took Shep for a walk in the fog? Describe the sensation of stepping off that curb when you didn't see it," he urged. At one point he'd considered being a journalist and enrolled in a few news writing classes at Los Angeles City College in the 1930s. However, architecture snagged his interest along with gymnastics and algebra, drawing and geometry, literature and hotel management. At the end of a few years he'd earned more than enough credits to graduate, with none of them adding up into any single major. "You can never run out of things to try," he once said. His favorite subject had been meteorology. He loved studying cloud formations and wind patterns, and he never tired of hearing about them. Most people talk about the weather when there isn't anything else to talk about. For my father it was the main topic.

He loved my Colorado reports of drops in temperatures. One time I called when it was five below zero; a few days later I phoned in a report that the thermometer now read four degrees. "A regular heat wave," he laughed. Today I can smell a storm coming. When one creeps down from the north on the scale of a blizzard, a scent precedes it like a faint white lily. Then the air turns sharp as if carrying millions of pointed triangles and it slants forward with a certain clarity.

I hardly do any winter chores without thoughts of Daddy. He would heartily approve of my working in a storm. He was that kind of a person.

Daddy was many people. He dazzled me as a child; and as daughters usually are with the first man they learn to love, I was truly smitten. Yet finding a way to piece together his unpredictable temper and his changeable levels of affection has not been easy. Peering through the bitter winds that later whipped between us requires finding compassion. He probably didn't understand the underlying cause of his behavior anymore than the rest of us do. And I've come to this: Some daddies spend entire lives trying to cross bleak inner landscapes with no ropes between the house and barn to guide them.

Nothing takes up an entire floor more than two dogs lying in front of a fire—snoring, paws twitching, the occasional whimper. Lady is the fretful sleeper. Is she chasing rabbits or running from something? She was eleven months old with a history of three homes by the time I gave her a warm, stable place to live. But years later she still wakes from a sound sleep and staggers over droopy eyed for a few endearing words. Then she turns around and goes back to her spot behind the couch where it's safe. An hour later she needs another pat on the head and more reassuring.

Emma, on the other hand, has no inkling life could be anything less than ideal. I brought her home barely weaned. Lady, being two years older, wasn't too keen on having a puppy around. I set Emma down on the floor and she nosed Lady's tummy then grabbed a teat with her tiny milk teeth. Lady made sure *that* foolishness would never happen again. Emma quickly settled in and never looked back.

Splotched black and white and gray in a mix of Australian Shepherd, Blue Heeler and Border Collie, Emma still doesn't quite know what to make of all this energy that seems to be hers. Thank goodness she doesn't know how smart she is. An email joke I read once about different dog breeds changing light bulbs had Border Collies not only changing the bulb but bringing the wiring up to code. Emma loves pleasing me so much she'd go a step further and dust the fixtures too. Lady is also part Aussie but sports a tail that curls over her back and her tongue is mottled pink and purple. Her genes carry a bit of Chow. This is the part that keeps her well-mannered but aloof. It's also the part that raised the hair on the back of my neck one day. As I sat on the mountainside with a view far down the canyon, Lady sat uphill but still nearby. Her tongue lolling to the side, her mouth smiling, she was a happy dog. Suddenly a slant of light caught a certain angle of her face and the Chow in her materialized like a uncanny shape-shifter. Goosebumps broke out on my arms. Her stubby nose morphed bestial, something to be very afraid of. Though a loving dog, Lady always maintained a fine line between us, one that held me back just a tad. After the day on the mountain I always respected the fact that she could easily bite the hand that feeds her.

America is gaga-eyed over dogs. For millions of people dogs have moved beyond protectors, even companions. Dogs are now full-blown members of the family; some even have places at the dining room table. The phenomenon started with dog psychologists then dog exorcists, dog acupuncturists, and now dog whisperers. Dog schools abound. Doggie day care is all the rage. People throw birthday parties complete with favors and party hats for their dogs. Once in a fashionable store in downtown Santa Fe all the clerks began a high-pitched cooing. An older woman had come in pushing a baby buggy. I glanced over expecting to see a baby, her grandchild perhaps. Instead, a tiny Pekinese wearing a bonnet and a white lacy dress sat in the middle of fluffy pink blankets.

Have people forgotten dogs evolved from wolves? In the DNA of every one of them, a decked-out Pekinese included, wildness isn't all that far away.

Today I stood before the fire warming my back side and inevitably Lady rolled on her back for a tummy rub. I obliged with my foot and loving words, saying she's a good girl. Knowing she was still loved, she flopped back over and went to sleep.

I envy the complete sleep dogs achieve almost instantly. I'm a restless sleeper, waking several times a night then getting up long before daylight. I've often lain awake next to lovers listening and watching them sleep. Fulton had fretful nights, fingers trembling, lips moving. His parents divorced when he was five, his mother whisking him away from the kindergarten playground one morning with no explanation. Just like that, snap, his father was gone. Fulton was like Lady, constantly needing reassurance. A crease of worry furrowed his forehead by day and was just as prominent when he slept.

Each year the assistant principal had singled out a strong, independent thinking female teacher to harass. He kept at her all year to the point where, completely worn down, she had no choice but to quit. I'd seen two great teachers go down. When my third year rolled around, I wondered who he'd target this time. It soon became obvious. Besides dropping by my classroom unannounced, he took to standing by the door every morning, clipboard in hand. If I wasn't inside when the bell rang, he'd make a great show of scratching with a mighty flourish on his notepad.

"Did you just get in trouble?" a rather perceptive boy asked one day.

"I believe I did."

That afternoon the assistant principal called me into his office. "Parents are complaining their kids don't have any homework in your classes," he smirked, like he'd finally gotten me. "They need to take home books."

I took a deep breath. "I don't use the textbooks because they are poorly written and confusing. I've developed my own practice sheets and that's what the kids take home."

He looked at me blankly. "They need to take home books."

So back to the classroom I went. "You all know I assign homework every night, right?" I said to each of my classes. "Well, I need to cut a deal with you." I explained the problem and said if they dutifully took home their books, I'd give them more time in class to read. This was when we were reading about Billy and his coonhounds.

"Cool!"

My classroom had a corner dedicated to pure reading, whatever the kids wanted. No tests, no book reports. Just reading. A donated patch of carpet topped with pillows contributed by parents made a cozy nook where you could curl up with a book. No adult would settle in with a book in one of those horrid classroom desks, yet we expect kids to. Equipped with a new degree as a Reading Specialist, I'd been hired to bring innovation to the classroom. But doing things the old way was the only way. Case in point: The kids could read fine. All they needed was more in depth comprehension. But I was told to teach phonics. When I balked, I was accused of insubordination. Is it any wonder the education in this country is sliding downhill? A secret school for administrators has to exist. How else do so many principals know how to break school-wide morale? Some are very good at it.

To find an inner balance amidst all this, I kept to my schedule of writing every day after work. The first draft was nearly done. Having a personal project in the works had raised my energy level, my tingling nerves were lessening, my hands less numb. Yet something loomed ominous. Fulton had taken to calling when he knew I was writing; he wanted me to meet him for drinks. Not later, now. It felt like a test, a test to see what was more important to me—him or writing to maintain my sanity. During one phone call he reminded me that he'd let me put a house on his land. I reminded him that I was still grateful. I was becoming frightened. Frightened of the rising price of being here.

I catch reflections of myself in mirrors and store windows. They startle me and I wonder what my mother is doing here. Sometimes my voice assumes the timbre of hers. I hear myself replying the way she would, using words that aren't mine. We chose very different paths in life, yet there are times when I feel the need to scrape her off of me, like her presence is a thin film covering my entire body. Finding the line that separated us hasn't been easy. Especially when it pertains to men. I never saw my mother express affection for my father. Coddling her husband was out of the question. Fussing over him unheard of. Often I watched her bring Daddy dessert while he watched television. Her face sagged with sourness. I learned to disdain the needs of men.

I learned men like sex but never learned they needed comforting. A man friend once said, "People think men want sex. What they really want is mothering."

Moments return when Fulton needed mothering, and I wasn't there. He gave a talk to a group and afterwards asked my impression. I said it was a hodgepodge. This didn't bode well with a man who needed lots of reassuring. Then I began coming home each day to at least five messages saying how much he missed me, how much he loved me. Panic filled me with all that he required. I couldn't give enough.

The school year began winding down, and the only thing that kept me going through the hectic days was another trip to the Caribbean that Fulton had planned. How I envisioned those sun-drenched days on the beach! I was looking forward to finally having some quality time with Fulton, away from all the niggling details in both our lives.

Right after final exams, the English chair called a department meeting. The first question was: "How can we get students to like reading?" The response was silence. Didn't anyone know? I spoke up: "Don't test them on everything they read." Even more silence followed, the kind that makes people squirm because they didn't want to hear such a simple truth. Testing was the only model the school had. The department chair gave a slight cough, nothing more was said, and we went on to other matters.

The next day I turned in grades and went home. The novel was done and feeling revived, I walked down to the river. I was looking forward to the summer. In two days we would board the plane. I'd bought a new beach outfit. My bags were packed. I couldn't wait. But that evening Fulton informed me I was excluded from our vacation. He said I hadn't been nice to him. Translated, this meant I hadn't given up my life, myself, and all my spare time for him. His announcement pushed our teetering relationship over the edge faster than anything else he could have said.

Three

If someone had tapped me on the shoulder and whispered that soon I'd be happily wandering the trails of mountain lions and bears, I wouldn't have believed a word. After the school year ended and Fulton left on our vacation, I felt paralyzed. Here I was stuck on land owned by a man who'd just kicked me in the teeth. I saw no way out. Then a most spectacular thing happened. The snow in the Sangre de Cristo Mountains started melting. The Pecos River flooded and as calamity tends to do, the event brought strangers together. I went down to watch the roiling waters with neighbors I'd never met. We gazed at the rising waters jumping the bank, pushing mud and branches headlong down the widened channel.

Every house along the river sat back from the bank nearly five hundred feet, a safe distance on higher ground. The old Hispanic families, whose ancestors settled here centuries before, knew this small stream—usually peaceful and harmless—could rage, flood, devastate, and kill. Those who still farmed kept pastures in the bottomland; no one lived close to the water. Except Fulton. His house sat forty-five feet from the waterway, and he boasted about having the only house close to the river.

I entreated the quickening waters to wash away every last vestige of his house. They didn't. Instead, while Fulton sipped sweet tropical drinks on warm white beaches, the rising waters began calling me. I went to the river in the morning. I went to the river in the afternoon. When a full moon filled the field in front of my house late one night, I carefully inched my way down to the banks. I needed the sound of running water.

One morning I headed for the river and decided to edge along the fence line closer to my house rather than using the steps that led from Fulton's house. In finding another way, I found another way.

The brambles grew thick. Being on a mission I went back to my house for a pair of garden snippers. A path appeared in no time. Though ragged and steep, it took me where I wanted to go: to the river. I walked along the muddy banks and noticed the river had gone down during the night. What the receding waters had left behind resembled a shipwreck. Logs and branches and old boards were jammed against trees and wedged into bushes. As I took in the scene, the smell of rot and decay rose from the dirty chaos. Always partial to jig-saw puzzles, I stood on the bank and idly wondered what it would take to untangle the mess the river had washed ashore.

Gingerly I unsnaked a twisted two-by-four from the grass. Next I unearthed a fence post mired in mud; with barbed wire still attached, it wasn't easy. I loosened some old boards pressed against a tree. I freed part of a weathered porch trapped between two cottonwoods. After each retrieval, I laid the pieces in the grass to dry and an hour later stood back to inspect my work. Suddenly it hit me. Of course! Right in front of me was a huge source of firewood.

Each morning I donned work gloves and wrangled boards and logs from the debris then hauled them up the steep path and across the field to my house. Sometimes I carried armloads of smaller branches. Other times I dragged one log at a time. Like a woman possessed I made at least two trips a day lugging this booty home.

Fulton called one afternoon cooing from half way around the world that he missed me. I let the ensuing silence hang heavily. He hurried on. He'd be home in two days and wanted to know the level of the river. He could have called the Forest Service but was really testing the waters, to see if I still wanted him. I didn't, but it would not be easy unraveling the nest I'd so longed to make. Yet I was beginning to learn how to do it: one board at a time.

Handling boards, rotten wood, and stacking lumber is something I grew up with. With the fireplace as our main source of heat, it always needed feeding. Many evenings when Daddy came home from the docks, he'd unload wood pieces from the trunk of the car. One of the benefits of working on wharfs is an endless supply of junk wood. Daddy scrounged the dumpsters for old planks. He salvaged end pieces of tongue and groove decking and saved bits of boards used to replace damaged hulls. He even lugged home pieces of those bottom-gray hulls. I loved the scraps of shiny leftover paneling from the fancy yachts. He worked on several boats owned by movie stars and the varnished pieces spoke of a lifestyle far beyond our means. What was close at hand, though, and easily within reach every winter was the woodpile behind our house. It was never low, the bin near the hearth never empty.

Now that I've come to know the efficiency of woodstoves, I understand Daddy's compulsiveness about collecting scrap wood. Fireplaces slurp most of the heat up the chimney and simultaneously pull cold air from every draft in the house. Every room except the living room was always cold. The fireplace required an excessive amount of wood.

When Fulton returned from his tropical trip, I was afraid if he saw me hauling logs from the river he'd say because the wood was on his land, it was his and I couldn't have it. So I waited until he left for work every morning before heading for the river. Grateful for a respite from the work-a-day world, at least for the rest of the summer, I loved this other universe. Just a short walk from the doublewide was a different climate thick with a humidity that brought dragonflies, mosquitoes, and many different species of butterflies. When evening came the swallows zipped through the air like tiny black bombers. A pair of long-legged blue herons paraded down the middle of the river every afternoon. If I sat on the shaded bank, they'd saunter by within several yards. If they spotted me, their ascent filled the air with that breathy sound of big wings flapping. One morning a golden eagle perched on a rocky ledge high above the river. The privilege of seeing that bird froze me in place.

Some of the river wood was so smooth and shiny I'd rub pieces against my cheek. I tucked one small polished knot with grain as intricate as a Celtic design into my pocket and smiled recalling my first lesson in driftwood. In my twenties I worked on a dude ranch in Arizona. Before the season opened the owner took the entire crew up a river canyon to look for driftwood. Being a beach girl I knew that driftwood could only be found near the ocean, so who did he think he was? Yet that day the desert revealed some lovely gnarled pieces of dried wood. No artisan could have made them any better. They looked like sculpted art, and by the end of our sun soaked day I had to concede that driftwood is any wood that drifts on any water.

A lot of years have passed since I hiked down those dry washes with the ranch crew, laughing and playing together. We hung from branches that arched over the banks. We scampered onto sandbars. I remember how agile my body was. Today when I set out for kindling, some days I need to stretch and bend a bit to loosen the joints. I'm over sixty now and too often every bone in my body aches. That summer along the river when I was dragging logs home, I didn't realize I was still young. I was forty-five. You can feel terribly old at any age if enough water washes you under enough bridges. My spirit that summer withered. I'd quit my job at the school. A friend got me a small landscaping job at a gallery in Santa Fe. What I'd do come fall I didn't know, and really didn't care. Right now my work was retrieving wood. The project lent focus; it structured my days. Dealing with wood is simple-minded and a powerful remedy for keeping the claws of depression from sinking too deeply.

So how does a woman finger her way out of hard times? I didn't know then and there's still nothing to trace like a definitive route. You end up following your nose, and trust that a wildcard is up a sleeve somewhere off to the side. My mother, who wasn't terribly pleased with how her life turned out, wasn't much help. I called one evening to talk over my situation and she reiterated one of her favorite lines: "Oh, something will come along. Everything always works out." Which is true, but only in retrospect. When you're in the midst of turmoil, a cliché doesn't offer much of a lifeline.

My mother was much better at navigating mountain terrain than finding a clear path through her own life. Even after I quit Girl Scouts, she continued leading expeditions along the John Muir Trail in the Sierra Nevada Mountains for girls who wanted a taste of wilderness. She was good at erecting make-shift shelters in unexpected storms but ill-equipped to console a daughter mired on some man's land. She'd remained stuck for so long in her own unfulfilling marriage that she probably didn't believe there were ways out. I wanted to reach through the phone and slug her.

Anger grows like a billowy dark cloud, uncontainable. It thrives on runaway thoughts that dredge up old fights, past injustices, your own stupidity. Fulton had promised to sell me half an acre; now he offered five feet of fallow land along the fence line. Rage is often mistaken for craziness. You can't think straight. You can hardly eat, or eat too much when you can finally keep food down. Over the summer, I watched Fulton bring home a string of women; one he paraded in front of my house walking arm in arm.

I continued reaching for gnarled branches and logs and dragging them home. From the outside I looked strong and able. I brushed mud-caked leaves from hollow logs and shook grass loose from drying planks. My arms muscled up, my legs tightened. My face tanned. However, for all this, I admitted to a friend that I'd stopped using sun block. "Is this a slow suicide?" she asked, knowing my past bouts with skin cancer. I gathered wood everyday until afternoon when, exhausted, I could sleep and forget. Then I'd wake the next morning feeling stuck again as if trying to move through a bay of brackish backwater. I had to push myself to go outside and hunt for more wood.

Four

Today, when I stand on my porch and gaze at the canyon wall, few remnants remain of those dark, livid days along the river. In fact, I caught sight of Fulton in a café not long ago. My response was simple: Oh, there's Fulton. And I continued on to the backroom. What relief that the racking anger was gone. What relief that no emotions whatsoever surfaced. When had all that dissipated anyway? Living among trees soothes the nerves as living near water does. Both absorb deep inner jaggedness and you don't even know an alteration has happened until wholeness starts feeling possible again.

There is a culture within trees that one can attune to. The constant aliveness puts troubles into perspective. Get into a quandary and trees help you know it's small, that it's passing. They lift then release hurt and cover wounds with their own solace. Trees give lessons in being still. They also teach everything changes, and change never holds back.

A few autumns ago, while scouting a good route for snowshoeing, I heard a sharp ripping and crashing too close for comfort and immediately looked up to see what was falling, which way to run. At first the sound reverberated like a rock shelf collapsing in a nearby canyon. Both dogs cowered next to my legs. After determining nothing was coming our way, I held my breath, listening. Not much time is needed for a tree to fall, which this had to be. They go with an impressive thunk. This wasn't my first time being in the vicinity of a downer. When all was quiet I hurried to inspect, the dogs close on my heels.

For years an old fir snag had been the topic of a friendly squabble between me and my neighbor Sloan. That we even got to a point where we talked was a milestone. Our friendship was slow in coming. After I'd lived here several years the battery in my car was dead one morning. I thought twice about asking him for help, he was such a recluse. He also worked nights driving a taxi in Santa Fe and slept during the day. I waited till noon to knock on his door. He was eager to lend a hand and as he hooked up a charger, we stood and talked. Another time I needed help getting a molasses jar lid open. I'd tried everything; this was before I took to keeping a set of channel locks in the kitchen drawer. I found Sloan grubby and greasy and lying on his back under one of his five VW bugs.

"Oh, hi. Let me roll on out of here. I'm always up for taking a break," he said and easily opened the jar. We chatted a bit before I went home to make ginger bread, later taking a piece over to him. Not long after that my mother died. I stayed two months in California, calling Sloan once or twice to check on things around my place. When I returned, we began sitting on one another's porches in the summer— "porching" as a girlfriend calls it. From the beginning we shared scraps from our lives. He was five years old when his aunt asked what he wanted to be when he grew up. Without missing a beat, Sloan said: "A hermit." His family flew into a tizzy. No, no. You can't be a hermit, they all cried. You need to be something. You need to do something.

"Isn't *being* a hermit *doing* something?" he now asks rhetorically.

One day I invited him to join me on a short hike. That was our beginning. We enjoyed tramping around in the woods together, and one day I showed him this long-standing dead fir tree, a snag with scraggily bare branches so high they appeared to be scratching the sky. The tree stood one hundred-fifty feet tall at least. Holes excavated by animals and birds proved that the inside was rotten. Whenever we passed it, we always debated how soon it would go down.

"I bet it goes tomorrow," I'd say.

"It'll be another twenty years," Sloan predicted.

"Nah," I countered, "it'll go any minute."

Now as the dogs and I skedaddled down the trail to Bear Canyon, I just had this feeling. We got there as the snag was still settling. On the way down it had taken out many smaller trees and the whole forest creaked and cracked and groaned for another twenty minutes. The tree now stretched across the arroyo and would have made a great bridge; but it broke at the bottom of the trunk leaving a few spikes of pulpy wood to catch on the upper bank. Everything about the scene looked unstable. The next day I brought Sloan to see the downer. We crossed to the other side of the canyon in search of the top of the snag.

"Look how it snapped in so many sections," he said. "It ripples up the slope like it was hinged." For weeks afterward we planned our treks to marvel at this tree, which served as a reminder that change lives constantly nearby. Whether you're living under trees or not.

I return again and again to downed trees as if journeying to sacred sites. The Indians in the Northwest have a tale about a big tree that's chopped down and as it falls, it breaks open the sky, and that's how it seems. The increased brightness that follows a downer is like a skylight has been installed. Whenever my dogs and I come across a newly fallen tree, it's always Emma that glances up. The freshly opened space grabs her attention. Lady, a bit closer to wild, sniffs the freshly turned earth, and pees. She knows we'll be back and appropriately marks our spot.

For many weeks each time I passed the downed snag, I let out a sigh, which told me how nervous the standing dead tree had made me. Now the danger was gone. After Papa South went down, I knew if a perfectly fine tree—at least from all appearances—could fall, could any tree go over any time? The answer was straightforward and for awhile I almost tippy-toed along the trails and caught myself ducking past certain trees. It's been years now and those same trees are still standing. But you never know.

A question kept returning after Papa South went down: Why this one and none of the others? Why hadn't I ever considered bringing home any of the other downed trees? That this tree had a name made a difference, except there was something else, and it seeped in one day when I came across a faded photo that my father had clipped from the newspaper. He squirreled away all kinds of odds and ends, which drove my mother nuts. She ranted about his pack rat ways, especially after he died. The piles he'd left behind were more tremendous than she suspected. Then when she died, I inherited the task of going through the rest of their belongings and brought home several boxes to sift through.

In much of the detritus my father left, I've been fortunate to glimpse snippets that help make sense of my own life. I'm sure Daddy didn't intend to leave behind assorted items that would fill in parts of my own story. He was merely a scrap-booker, though nothing got pasted down. Nothing was organized.

During the two years I let Papa South season on the mountainside, I began going through the boxes I'd lugged home. I wasn't present at Daddy's death. I'd written a letter holding him accountable for the mayhem he had caused our family. Word came back that he railed against me on his death bed. I've never regretted not being at his side when he died. Still, I was able to rummage through his cartons of stuff with sentiment, longing, and tenderness. No relationship is solidly one way. The old photo Daddy had clipped from the local paper was of a tree that had fallen on our street. Unfolding the newspaper clipping, I immediately remembered what a big deal that tree going down had been in the neighborhood. I was in kindergarten. What I hadn't realized was how deeply the incident had wedged inside of me.

A Santa Ana wind was blowing that day. This is an eerie warm wind coming off the Mojave Desert, the kind of wind that makes your skin crawl, the kind that makes people want to kill each other, and sometimes do. During high winds, large fronds ripped from palm trees, and branches and needles dropped from the pine trees. On this particular day as the school bus drove down our street I saw lots of pine cones on the sidewalks. Getting off the bus at the next corner, I ran home and told Mama that I was going to look for pine cones.

Several pine trees grew in front of our house and I headed for the biggest one. I walked beneath it and squatted down, putting various sized cones into a pile. I chose one and started back toward the house to douse it with glue and gold glitter. Not more than ten feet from the tree I heard a ripping sound behind me. I turned and the tree fell. Just like that. The tree I'd been playing under was stretched across the street, its top most branches lying on the corner of a neighbor's roof.

I stood in awe. Perfectly still, I stared at the tree as though in a dream. I hadn't sucked my finger in years; it went into my mouth now. I'd never been in the face of such power and stood transfixed. This was solemn business, this tree falling and me being the only one to see it go down. When two beings share a moment, they're fastened together, forever. The spell broke when my mother came shrieking down the sidewalk. "Oh, my god. Are you alright?"

I calmly looked up at her and mumbled around my finger, "A tree fell."

I held the faded clipping of the fallen tree for a long moment before folding and placing it back in the box with my father's other keepsakes. That huge tree lying across the street had been a momentous occasion. When word got around that a tree was down, kids arrived from up the street. They came from around the block, from across town. This was the most exciting thing that had happened in a long time. When the photographer from the local newspaper arrived, we all scrambled up on the thick trunk. There was a lot of shoving among the older boys, a lot of shouting and laughter. Yet a part of me sagged. It was my tree. I'd seen it topple over and in all the commotion that fact was not known.

When the photographer told us all to huddle closer, I remember urgently telling some of my playmates that I saw it go down. I implored, "I saw it fall." Finally a sharp mouthed little girl retorted, "So what?" and scampered up a branch like she owned the thing. I remember smiling real big for the photographer; after all, this was my tree even if no one knew it.

That incident, buried in cellular memory, must have jolted loose after finding Papa South because the first item on my to-do list was telling my neighbor Rodger that I had first dibs. It was my tree. He is forever cutting trees on his place, revving up his wood splitter, and stacking the wood neatly in rows between trees. He makes it more than a hobby. He is as obsessed with wood as I am, something I realized several years after moving here.

I had come home from town tired late in the afternoon and settled on the couch with a book. Leaning back, it occurred to me that more sunlight than usual brightened the living room. I looked up and saw an unprecedented full view of the canyon wall. What was going on? I peered out the window, my eyes opening wide. A huge ponderosa, at least seventy feet high on my property had lost a gigantic branch—in Rodger and Julie's yard. I ran outside, and my mouth dropped open. The ponderosa on my neighbor's place on the other side of me had also lost a huge branch—in my yard. On closer inspection, these were double-trunked trees, ones that years ago had split and grown two trunks.

Sometimes the canyon becomes a funnel with winds whooshing straight through, often bending trees to the breaking point. The wind that day, I later heard from those who'd seen it, resembled a tornado. When the neighbor on the other side of me, got home and saw the wreckage, she washed her hands of her tree in my yard. "Oh, you can have the wood," she said. As if it's that simple. However, when it came to Rodger things were different.

A week before, I'd been pruning various trees on my place, mostly the cedars that suck up water from the leach field and go crazy putting out new growth every year. With the high fire conditions in the past few years, Rodger, Julie, and I are forever clearing brush from around our houses. They also have a house in Albuquerque and the weekend before had brought up a wood chipper.

"If you want, just throw your branches over the fence and we'll chop them up," Rodger offered. Great. I had a growing pile.

The day the big trunk fell off, I called them. The next day Rodger was already sawing off branches when I returned from town. "Hey, remember when I said you could toss your branches over the fence? I think you overdid it." His words were rhetorical and, luckily, full of good humor. The branch had smashed their fence.

"You're cutting up my tree," I wailed only half in jest.

Rodger smiled and lifted his chainsaw in salute. "Finder's-keepers." And he went back to work.

After that high wind the forest looked like some woodland giant had strolled along willy-nilly snapping ponderosas like toothpicks. Oddly enough most of them were double-trunked trees like the ones in our yards; odder still, all the trunks that broke were on the northern side of the tree. It was a wind with a mission.

Split-trunked trees happen when browsing deer, raccoons, or porcupines nibble the fresh tops off saplings. These tops are the leader growth, the highest point on a tree. If they get eaten, a tree needs to respond quickly in order to survive. Automatically one of the lateral branches, a side branch, becomes the leader; and without skipping a beat, the tree goes right on reaching for light despite having been eaten. Trouble starts when two lateral branches become leader. The tree gets twice the amount of sunlight and grows too quickly.

When pen pal Bernd Heinrich published *The Trees in My Forest*, the book became my manual for watching individual trees as well as an entire forest. Bernd has a perceptive eye with wide-ranging insights. Though the trees that cover his three hundred acres in Maine are different varieties than the ones here in the Southwest, their behavior is similar. Of the conical shaped seed-bearing trees around his cabin, he concluded that conifers with two heads were worse off than others because when both want to be leaders, the tree suffers. In their competitive grab for sunlight both branches weaken the overall health of the tree. They stress the entire system—especially the spot where the first nibbling took place, where the two lateral branches began angling upward. With split leader growth the nutrients that the roots pull up sometimes aren't enough for two trees; consequently, the tree from the split on up gets drained. Neither branch is at full potential.

Eventually a heavy snow or wind breaks one of them off.

Five

Scientists uncovered the earliest fossils of *Pinus ponderosas* in Nevada. They dated back 600,000 years. Ponderosa fossils 100,000 years old have been found in Yellowstone. By the time people began migrating into North America between 15,000 and 30,000 years ago these trees had already established their niche. Typically, the ponderosa thrives in arid habitats that receive about fourteen inches of rain a year and depending on climate patterns, stands of ponderosas tend to drift. Records show that the central part of New Mexico once supported the ponderosa; now that same area is prairie grasslands.

The first documented use of ponderosa in the Southwest dates to 100 A.D. when the Pueblo ancestors used small logs to support roofs of pit houses, partially underground rooms covered with grass, sticks, and mud. Later their large communal structures rose to five stories with ponderosa logs supporting the overhead construction. The best-known site is Chaco Canyon, located in northwestern New Mexico. At the height of their civilization (between 900 and 1125) they used 150,000 ponderosa logs as roof beams for their houses and subterranean ceremonial rooms, the kivas. There's evidence of an extensive network of roads, but the big question still remains: How did these people get all those logs down from mountains fifty to sixty miles away—without horses, without wheels? Did they work in teams and carry them? Did they roll them down the roads? The theories that archeologists continue tossing around are speculative at best.

Ponderosas are huge trees. With good reason their name comes from the Latin word for "ponderous." A fresh-cut log twenty-seven inches thick and fourteen feet long weighs a ton. Well, Papa South was a lot longer and rounder and nothing other than clever engineering was ever going to get this tree out. When I finally told Rodger that this Papa South tree was finder's keepers, he didn't put up one inch of fight. He merely shrugged and said okay like he was relinquishing a good deal, but what could he do? Then he paused before asking:

"Have any idea how you're going to get it down?"

The next day hiking near the forest road way up on the mountainside, I watched four pickups caravan down the steep dirt road. In the bed of each truck was a load of freshly cut ponderosa. Two men rode in each cab and each one looked exhausted. A truck would never get up to Papa South. I'd have to haul this log out some other way. No matter what, the task would be difficult.

No, I had no idea how I'd get it down.

No doubt it was my father who instilled my innate tendencies for making dibs on wood. His father died during the flu epidemic in 1918, when my father was seven years old. His mother found work as the school janitor and by all standards my father and his little brother grew up poor. He often reminisced about the coal wagon making deliveries. "After it left, I'd pick up every last scrap of coal that had fallen and I'd chase after the wagon to get anything that dropped off," he told me once. Daddy turned into a great scavenger and with no shame attached to his early circumstances, he continued foraging for just about anything. On trash day he'd head for the alley behind our house to check out the neighbors' cans before setting off for the docks. Occasionally, in the summer I'd go with him and we'd bring home all kinds of neat stuff. I found a small rag doll once and the next week a perfectly good wooden box the right size for her bed.

When my sister first married, she grandly showed her new husband a big umbrella with a curved wooden handle that she found down the alley from their apartment. In mint condition and finished with a thick varnish, it was very English. Her husband was deeply humiliated realizing he'd married a woman who thought nothing of pawing through other people's trash.

My father was philosophical about the practice: "You never know what's there until you find it." Over the years I've brought home chairs, tables, sweaters, and books. Once driving down Canyon Road in Santa Fe I spied a three-foot high colorfully painted ceramic donkey standing among trash bins. I've regretted ever since passing it up.

My first lessons in scavenging for wood reach back to the cool, foggy California days after Christmas. Throughout the week leading up to New Years, our father gave me and Cathy permission to completely scour the alleys. He wanted us to bring home all the discarded Christmas trees we could find. My best friend Chris joined our expeditions, and the three of us set out every morning and made another sweep later in the afternoon. We'd revel in the cry: "There's one!" It was fierce competition, spotting those trees. "Dibs on that one!" We'd drag them home by the wooden stands, bits of tinsel leaving a silver trail down the streets and sidewalks. We brought the trees into our small bricked patio.

As the week went on, we pushed and shoved the trees to make them fit. It looked like a Christmas lot of rejected trees. By then the needles were drying and most of the trees leaned sideways. The wooden stands weren't all that sturdy and by the time we got them home some of the trees refused to stand upright anymore. We smashed them together, fitting in as many as possible. One time we counted thirty-five trees. The scent that wafted from all those pines made the foggy days smell clean and fresh. The overall picture was a little depressing, though; a make-shift forest seriously out of whack. But when Daddy came home each evening and saw the number of new trees, the delight on his face made the effort worthwhile.

He wanted the trees for the wood and took to them with a practiced hand. Lifting a hatchet he'd whack whack whack, and each spindly branch easily sliced off. Then he'd hack hack hack on the trunk angling cuts one way; he'd shift the hatchet and hack hack hack the other way, making a deep V-cut. In one quick motion he snapped the trunks across his knees into fireplace lengths. One time he showed me how to use the hatchet only my hands were too small. But the lesson accumulated somewhere because years later when time came to chop kindling, I knew the moves. How long it took for those Christmas trees to season, I'm not sure. Air is moist by the ocean and dampness settles into wood deeply. While the supply lasted, though, there were plenty of warm, sparkly fires. I was quite young when learning about the security of woodpiles.

Of course the other side of scavenging is never throwing anything away. My father kept bundles of snarled string and bits of wire, stubs of countless pencils, rubber bands, jars and jars of pennies. He also kept stacks of old newspapers. An open shelf a foot wide ran near the ceiling above the dining room. He designed the house, and I've often wondered if he actually intended that ledge for storing newspapers. They fit perfectly and over the years the papers added up as Daddy tucked them away for safe keeping—safe for what we never knew.

Periodically my mother would get on a tear, curse my father's pack-rat ways, rummage through his "collections," and try to clean them up. One time she got a ladder and enlisted the help of me and Cathy, handing down layers of newspapers from the dining room ledge. No one said a word when we sat down to dinner that night. Then Daddy happened to glance up and didn't speak to my mother for three days.

Daddy rarely allowed anything to get away from him. "You never know when it might come in handy" was his motto. One time in my teens I devised a sculpture project and needed some round wooden plugs, the remains of holes bored through boards. Did he have anything like that? I could always count on Daddy having anything a person would ever need, tucked away somewhere. After hearing what I wanted, he shifted in his chair and glared at my mother. The week before she'd insisted that he throw something away. "I kept a bag of wooden plugs for twenty years. Last week I threw it out." He paused only for a moment before continuing with a piece of advice. "Never throw anything out because the next day you'll need it."

So I come by it honestly—those stacks of wood out back, stacks of wood out front, and stacks along every side of the house. The collection grows by any number of means. On assignment a number of years ago for an article about a local sawmill, I spied a great stack of wood that couldn't be passed up.

Located outside Santa Fe, the sawmill is called Spotted Owl Timber. The owner David Lindsey told me, "My brother suggested the name. It was sorta tongue-in-cheek, but I decided to go with it."

Spotted Owls. The bane of loggers but a career benchmark for Eric Forsman, a wildlife biology undergraduate at Oregon State University. In the summer of 1968 he took a fire lookout job and while on duty noticed two owls he'd never seen. He went on to study spotted owls and their symbiotic relation with old growth Douglas-firs, establishing that ancient forests are where these birds nest, raise their young, and live out their lives. Forests also provide an abundance of squirrels and voles and other rodents to sustain the owls. In 1973 the Endangered Species Act got passed and Forsman made sure the Mexican Spotted Owl was on the list. At the time only one hundred of their nests were accounted for. Until his findings the old-growth Douglas firs were ruthlessly harvested for lumber. That one bird has stopped entire logging operations throughout the West.

The irony for this small independent sawmill is most of the logs that pass through the whirring blades are Douglas fir, most from private lands. Conducting a tour of his place, Lindsey took me into an area filled with large bundles of wood that looked like scrap, odds and ends from the milling process.

"Can people buy those?" I asked.

"We can't wait for people to take them," he said.

The next day I borrowed Sloan's pickup and arrived at the sawmill before noon. I dickered with a yardman about which pile, what price, and struck a deal. The stacks were bound with inch-wide metal strapping. A crane lifted the bundle, and I held my breath as the wood lowered into the truck. Thank goodness it was a three-quarter ton; even so, the creaking as the rough-cut wood settled didn't sound all that reassuring.

Driving back home I fit right in with an old rural New Mexico tradition. Sloan's truck is a classic. Part Ford, part Chevy, and mottled with dents and rust, it trundled along at about thirty miles an hour. The creaking of the load meant don't push it. So I sat back and enjoyed the scenery. Not enough of us get an outing in a dilapidated truck anymore. People honked and flipped me off as they zipped by in their spiffy SUVs. Newcomers no doubt. They just didn't know this is how it's supposed to be: lugging wood home in an old beat up truck. You take it slow, the old-timey way.

Once back home, I asked the kid next door to help unload it. In an hour I had a majestic pile of wood. At $15 dollars, it was a steal.

You'd think a pile of wood is just that: a pile of wood. But around my place (and ask anyone who gathers wood) each pile has a story. No matter what, every pile whether split or not and designated as junk or scrap contains a thread of narration. I was fussing around in the yard a few years ago when a truck pulled up. It was Joe and his wife Barb, a couple who, right after I bought my place, bought one of the cabins around the corner from me. In the process of remodeling it for a rental, they ripped out everything that could be ripped out— doors, windows, walls, counters, floors. On their way to the dump they pulled up to say hi.

"Have anything you want thrown out?" they asked. Offers of dump runs don't come very often so I scurried around gathering garbage, ashes, and cardboard boxes. As I threw the stuff in the back of their truck, something caught my eye.

"You guys taking those old boards to the dump?" I asked.

"You want them?"

After that they began leaving old wooden parts with me as a matter of course. Another time Barb told me I could have a bunch of old wood under the porch. Goodie. I lugged it all home.

My friends Peggy and Dodge spent seven years building their own house. For the next twenty years Dodge continued repairing and adding on, which meant lots of scrap lumber. When they eventually exchanged their woodstove for a pellet stove (much to their disappointment), I became the lucky recipient of all that scrap wood. Dodge brought over pickup loads, trailer loads, and barrel loads of end pieces. His arrivals always made me dance that little jig. Another delivery of wood is another measure of security. More is always welcome.

A few years ago someone highly recommended one of the roadside guys. "He sells really good oak," my friend said. Against all better judgment, I decided to give it a try. The guy showed up in his rickety truck and unloaded the cord.

"You sure this is dry?" I asked. It looked a little suspicious.

"Yeah, it's been on our land for several years," he said then left, no doubt chuckling the whole way. The wood was so green I had to let it sit for several years on my own land. I always hated the way that wood behaved in the fire. It never seemed to burn, only smolder, and I looked for all kinds of ways to get rid of that wood. Some of it got put to use as a low edging around the garden. Some of it literally became a house-warming present when a friend moved into a place with a woodstove. She reported later how the dying embers from the oak added to the ambiance of the house. I brought her more.

I'll never forget that load of oak. Mostly I hated the way the guy lied to me. The wood had been on his land for several years, all right. In the form of standing trees. The last piece wasn't gone soon enough.

Six

This afternoon I fired up the chainsaw and spent two hours out in the yard cutting cedar logs. While stacking my latest load of cordwood, many sections of cedar were too long for my stove so I tossed them off to the side. Usually I get the short pieces; not sure what happened this time. But I don't mind halving them. With cedar, though, sometimes there's a catch in the wood and the chain wants to bind up. It's tempting to back off, but the only way out is through. Put on some pressure, keep the saw going. Between cuts I noticed the switch was sticking and wondered if this tool is on its last legs. It's the same one I bought when living along the river, after lugging home all the leftovers from the flood.

When the pile of driftwood was good and high that summer, I went to Sears and bought an electric chainsaw. Lightweight, the blade not terribly long or unwieldy with a chain easy to tighten and replace, the tool was perfect. When I got home, I draped an extension cord out the backdoor, plugged in the chainsaw, and from the moment I pressed "on" something in me shifted.

A chainsaw is an empowering piece of equipment. A stripe of self-sufficiency never known before suddenly showed up. I grabbed it instantly. Having my own chainsaw opened more possibilities than ever imagined. Especially when I turned each log into Fulton's head. Especially after finding a note he'd left on my car saying an old friend popped in to say hello, that I'd really like her, so come on down and have breakfast with them. I glued the note in my journal as one more piece of evidence that my dreams were disintegrating, as if more testimony were needed.

What a joy cutting river wood! Touching a whirring chain to dry, bleached logs is like slicing warm butter. The saw glides with no binding, no hesitation. The feel is most gratifying, the work pure pleasure. I reserved the cool mornings for sawing and woke each day knowing the order of things. Humidity settles heavily along a river and even under the shade of the apple trees, I sweated easily as I tackled the jumble of driftwood. For the rest of the summer I built up a good-sized pile of wood ready to burn. It grew and grew. Then a teaching job turned up at a private boarding school for learning disabled teens. Located fifteen miles from my house up the Pecos Canyon, the job couldn't have been better. School started after Labor Day.

Before class one morning the door flew open as sixteen-year-old Susie burst through. She was a kid with a knack for knowing everything about everyone at all times. Breathless and full of drama, she cried out: "There's a kitten in the nurse's cabin. It just showed up. You better go get it. *Now!*"

I'd mentioned in passing to some of my classes that one of these days I'd like to get a cat. Leave it to Susie to personally assume the task of finding one. During the lunch hour we journeyed together to check out this wayward creature.

New batches of gray kittens periodically showed up at the school. They'd wander in from the forest and most were wide-eyed and manic, hardly the cuddling type. Nevertheless, lolling on the top bunk in the infirmary was a fluffy gray kitten about three months old. Emanating from this long-haired fuzz ball was a purr that rivaled an outboard motor. This wild thing didn't mind one bit being handled. Totally smitten I took the kitten home to the doublewide and chose the name Amy before learning it was a boy. Oh well. On special occasions, he became Mr. Ames.

Working at the boarding school made living in the doublewide somewhat bearable. By late October a friend found me a rent-free place to live in Santa Fe. "The woman is going to Brazil and won't be back for two years. Her place is the last house on a dead-end street," he said. I knew the area; several blocks had turned into a like-minded community that threw impromptu dinners and poetry readings. It was tempting. "The house even has a kiva fireplace." Now he was trying to appeal to my senses. He almost succeeded. My name wasn't on the papers for the doublewide. My credit hadn't been good at the time so Fulton really owned it, though I'd scrabbled together the down payment. However, I never made an attempt to change the deed once my credit got reestablished. I'd seen the writing on the wall. Essentially I could walk away. I took a long evening to decide.

Kiva fireplaces, one of those quaint Southwestern novelties that make newcomers so giddy with the charm of it all, are bee-hive style fireplaces tucked into corners. They do look cozy and have all those historical connotations of originating in the old pueblos. Most kiva fireplaces, however, are hardly better than a candle when it comes to throwing out heat. They're also like any other fireplace and slurp all the heat up the chimney. Here I was in front of a fire with slow flames licking the glass door of my woodstove, a cat curled on my lap, books and pillows piled all around me. My little prophet Lisa had spoken well. Rising early before work and making a fire had become routine. Each day ended with a walk to the river then a long evening before the fire reading and writing. If I returned to city life, finding a way back to any of this would prove too difficult, and may not happen at all.

Just then a log fell into the dying flames and a fantasy village emerged. Gazing into fires through glass doors is as meditative as watching clouds, and no less fanciful. As I watched the twinkling lights in that little village with a winding street past glittering shop windows, a deep orange glow tinted the darkened room. Amy snuggled deeper against me and the flirtation with a small house on a dead-end street began to recede. The love of a woodstove and the sanctuary that fires offer kept me from moving and helped me endure one more year on Fulton's land.

I'd trusted the promise of that Detroit coat once; I would continue trusting that the road wasn't over. Something would come along. It always does.

Hearthside

*T*HIS MORNING I WOKE TO THREE INCHES of snow and the scene out the window couldn't be prettier. The little tufts of white on the tips of evergreen branches are exactly what I pleaded for so long ago. A flocked tree. No matter how much my sister and I begged, Daddy refused to get us a flocked tree for Christmas. They were all the rage and everyone had one. "That white stuff will get all over the house," he protested.

Not getting what you want makes for a powerful incentive so during the week before New Years we scoured the alleys like detectives on the move. Spotting a flocked tree turned the moment festive and we'd drag it home, leaving a white trail of white stuff behind us. Cathy and I were thrilled with each flocked tree standing in our patio. I still marvel that you nearly always get what you wish for, though it may not arrive in the form you envisioned. Like how the detour around Papa South came about.

I walked up Slow and Easy where Papa South laid stretched out and drying in the sun, and something felt different. I stood and pondered things for a bit. That Rodger. It had to have been him. He and I are the only ones who tend to forest matters here. He'd moved a few limbs out of the way, scraped a narrow footpath through the pine needles, and already had a bypass around the stump. Geez, why hadn't I thought of that? Now I wouldn't have to cross the arroyo and wind through the brambles to get back to the trail. Jog a bit to the left and you'd be on your way. Another wish in another form.

"Hey, thanks for making that detour," I said next time we met up.

"You sure were going to a lot of trouble cutting through all that brush. Any thoughts yet on how you'll get that tree down?"

No, but the answer was simple: Somehow it would happen.

One

A small wicker valise sits high on a shelf in my office. Every so often I take it down and gently slide open the bamboo latch. Bundled by date starting with 1928 and continuing to 1950 are one hundred-fifty-four letters. Many years ago on the morning I was to catch a plane back home after visiting my mother, she held out a basket and said, "This is for you. I thought you might like it."

"What's in it?" I asked.

"Oh," she waved her hand in the air like it was nothing. "They're letters your father wrote to his mother. When your grandmother died, your aunt got the letters. When your father died, Aunt Lou sent them to me."

Daddy had died five years before and this was like finding an heirloom in an old forgotten attic. At the time the nation was weeping through *The Bridges of Madison County*. How I longed to find a diary tucked away in some old trunk. As I carefully lifted the top of the basket, my mother said, "Your father liked to write, you know." Yes, he was the one who instilled my love of language. I also craved anything to do with the family story. Inside I danced that little jig again. What a find!

I carried that wicker case through the airport and onto the plane and tucked it under the seat close to my feet. I'd only seen my grandmother once, when I was five. She died shortly afterwards. Daddy had left home the day after he graduated from high school and hit the road. I didn't know that for twenty years he had sent his mother letters. When I returned to the doublewide, I spread the letters all on the floor to organize them. Amy of course wanted to help, the way cats do. He rolled around on top of the envelopes, grabbing corners, and biting them. Finally, I bundled each year with a ribbon. Then I created a special pouch by covering the logo on a bank's money bag with duct tape and wrote "Letters" on it. Every morning for the next month I inserted the next three letters and carried them to work. Between classes, even in class when the kids were reading, I took out the next letter. Eating my lunch without one of Daddy's letters propped in front of me was impossible.

As a kid, I used to wonder how my father could strike up a conversation with anyone and so easily find common ground. Whether it was someone strolling down the sidewalk in front of the house or standing ahead of us in line at the movies, my father's small talk coaxed people to open up. How did he do this? Reading the letters I began to see he just had the knack. Each evening I curled up in my chair in front of the fire with the next installment like anticipating another chapter in a long novel. Reading the letters created an odd juxtaposition because the main character was someone I thought I knew; however, the letters gave a glimpse of a young man who was a complete stranger.

In the summer of 1928, at age seventeen, my father left Middleton, Michigan with a buddy. They set out to see the world and landed in Detroit. His buddy soon trundled back home, leaving my father to head east to Muskegon where he found work in a department store, roomed in a boarding house, then took a job in a piston factory making forty cents an hour. The crew went on strike for fifty cents and he felt compelled to show his solidarity. "I was sorry to go because I liked my job…but I would be ashamed to look the old crew in the face if I had showed a yellow streak and didn't quit," he wrote.

In a letter dated July 8, 1929 he tells his mother not to be surprised if the next letter isn't from Muskegon. "I may travel a little bit this year." Restlessness was setting in.

July 16, 1929
Well, Ma, here I am, way out West in Kansas working
in the harvest fields. Got a lift with a trucker straight
through to Ohio. Maybe I'll get me a job driving trucks.

August 4, 1929
I'm in south central Idaho. Tomorrow we'll be cutting grain
with a team of 18 mules. I always wanted to be a cowboy.

August 28, 1929
This hauling wheat sacks is the bunk . . . I expect to get a sheep
herding job up here in the Idaho hills.

Instead, he ended up in Oregon working in the hops fields then he picked peaches before heading for central California where relatives lived. After a few days of clowning around with cousins he hadn't seen in ages, my father went on to Los Angeles—a week before the stock market crashed.

Daddy told tales around the dinner table of hopping freight trains on his way west. This wasn't mentioned in the letters, probably to spare his mother. Letter after letter ended with, "Don't worry." Young and eager, he followed the open road and gathered all kinds of stories to tell again and again over the years. Though his story was personal, historically he joined 250,000 young people between the years 1929 and 1939 that left home during the Great Depression. Most were between the ages of sixteen and twenty-five; all were in hope of finding work. In droves they began fanning across America.

Somewhere in the back of my mind, I always thought Daddy would up and leave for the open road again. Our home life couldn't compare to his wild stories. But I learned one day that adventure can be found right in your own backyard.

When I was nine years old, we were driving down the main highway in town. Suddenly Daddy braked and said, "Look at that!" Two Mexican women sat crying on a bus bench. Daddy pulled up along the curb and got out. The women spoke no English; my parents knew a smattering of Spanish and figured out the bus had dropped them off in Corona del Mar instead of Corona, another town far inland in a whole other direction.

The women were lost and didn't know what to do. Daddy told me and my sister to scoot over so the women could get in the backseat. My mother fixed a stupendous lunch and the conversation turned lively through a mixture of two different languages. My father fairly dazzled. From my vantage point fifty years later, the open road had happened for him once again right in his own home. After determining the correct bus schedule, Daddy drove the women to the station. Long ago strangers had taken him in, offering food and shelter, and pointed him down the road. He was only returning the favor.

Somewhere along the way I acquired a deep curiosity about people, the seed planted, no doubt, by watching my father. After maneuvering out of teaching and returning to journalism, I was in the middle of interviewing a woman for a business profile for the local paper. She suddenly stopped and said she didn't want an article after all, and sent me away. Later the editor called, laughing. "That woman said you asked too many questions," he said. I have a fascination with people—where they come from, how they get from there to here. Detours, side trips, and unrealized dreams fill any narrative with depth. That a jeweler used to be a champion surfer, that a high-end shoe designer feeds stray cats in her neighborhood only add to the human side of a story, even a piece for the business section. To get the backstory you have to ask questions. It's like collecting wood. You gather the tidbits of people's lives then stack them in such a way that warms people's hearts.

Two

Today Andrew is coming with my yearly load of cordwood. Gone are the days of workmen tossing out each piece one by one. A few years back Andrew showed up in a shiny new rig, hopped out, and said, "Hey, do you like my new truck? Watch this." He pressed a button that raised the back of his truck. Two cords of split piñon and cedar slid into my driveway. When I wrote out the check the cost of that new truck was clearly embedded in the higher prices. "Remember when a cord of wood was $50?" I grumbled, handing him a check for $500.

"Those were the days," he agreed, not about to relinquish even a piece of that nice fat check. Yet the price also includes going further afield to find that wood. When sources for piñon began dwindling locally, Andrew began sending crews to Gallup, at least five hours away to harvest trees on private land. Today he contracts to have the trees delivered to his woodlot. So every year I write a check that keeps Andrew in business and me in wood. Handing over a good chunk of money is the price I pay to feed a woodstove that loves eating every piece of wood I can get my hands on. The exchange means I don't have to go into the forest to cut it myself and don't have to haul it home, and I don't have to deal with the guys by the road.

One time I borrowed a truck and loaded wood myself at Andrew's. He made sure it was stacked. "When wood is just tossed into a truck, it loses fifty-percent of volume," he reminded me. He also says a typical pickup, even when tightly packed, is a third of a cord. But people still call it a cord. The panels on Andrew's new truck were designed to measure full cords and he can haul three. It's always an impressive sight to see him drive up my road with wood.

A month after moving to the forest, I called Andrew for my annual delivery of wood and gave directions. He got out, stood with his hands on his hips, and without saying a word slowly surveyed the trailer, the yard, the rubble that would eventually become a flower garden. After scanning the dilapidated chicken coop, his eyes went further afield to the canyon wall. He turned and took in the surrounding forest. Finally he spoke.

"I've seen a lot of places, but this is the prettiest yet. I think you made a wise move."

And the choice to settle here wasn't even difficult.

Still living in the doublewide when spring came around, I started an exercise regimen of walking each morning before work. My route took me up the canyon a mile and back. Each morning a small gray

pickup drove by, coming down the canyon probably heading into Santa Fe. The driver and I would nod or wave in that country folk way.
Then I began gearing up to move, sorting and packing belongings.
There was no plan, other than wanting to stay in Pecos. The drive
to and from the boarding school each day had deepened a fondness
for the canyon. The two lane road wound through thick forest and
open meadows. Close to the school the road nearly got swallowed by
shadow in a narrow cut through steep granite cliffs. If only I could live
in the canyon with its rhythms, its changing scenery. This could make
up for leaving the river bottom. To and from work, I began looking
for property. Nothing grabbed me until my eyes were drawn to one
particular dirt road.

"A for-sale sign should be there," I muttered to myself one afternoon. Each day I'd stare and stare as if trying to conjure up a sign.
"Where is it?" Three days later it appeared: a for-sale sign at the entrance to the road. An old singlewide sat under tall ponderosas and
the man selling was the driver of that small gray pickup. Some things
are that simple, and we're still friends.

I was sorry to leave the river but relieved to be out of the doublewide and all that it signified. I didn't miss any of the implications moving here: a singlewide for a single life. Things were looking up. Even
Amy was amenable to the change. He'd come from the forest so was
perfectly at home here. I lost him several years later when friends in
town watched him while I was on vacation. He slipped out the door
and never came back.

I'd had to leave Luke with Fulton. With no fences up yet, it wasn't
wise to take her with me. This was hard. She preferred being with me.
But one day I brought Luke to my new place and kept her overnight.
The next morning I took her furry face in my hands, told her to find a
way to come back, that I loved her.

A week later I dreamed Luke was trying to find me, wandering aimlessly. All the next day an uncanny feeling persisted that she was nearby, almost touching me. Then word came for me to call Fulton. I hadn't given him my new number. He had left Luke in his girlfriend's fenced yard. Somehow Luke had gotten out and tried crossing Cerrillos Road, the busiest street in Santa Fe, and didn't make it. She had indeed tried finding me. Luke's death held purpose, though. She severed the last thread between me and Fulton.

After Andrew dropped off my first load of wood here in the forest, I made my usual trip to his place for kindling. A week later as I poked along the edge of the forest looking for an entrance, my good fortune suddenly dawned on me. No longer would it be necessary to drive to the woodlot for scraps. A never-ending supply of kindling was right here—right in front of me, right before my very eyes. Just like the driftwood along the river. The following year when Andrew delivered my wood he said: "You don't come for kindling anymore."

No, now I go into the forest.

After so many years my system for getting the small stuff is in place. It began during "the winter of lots of snow" when the twigs and branches I retrieved were too damp to bring into the house. They needed to sit on the porch in the carrying bags "perking up"—what I call drying out. A routine developed after I bought another green carrying bag. When one satchel was empty, I went for another load. During winters of lots of snow there is always a perk pile on the porch. The carrying bags never sit idle for long.

During one gathering expedition, the dogs and I got a rush of adrenalin only a few minutes after setting off. The previous day I'd piled some downed limbs and wanted to bring them home. As the dogs trotted ahead, warming up for their usual ten miles to my one, a series of coyote yelps erupted from behind a low rise. Both dogs took off at a dead run. Coyotes, ever the tricksters, seem to throw their voices around like ventriloquists making it hard to tell how many are in a pack or where they are. I had no idea how this would turn out so stopped and held my breath.

Emma was the first to come barreling back down the path. Breathing hard, hackles raised, eyes wide, her expression asked: "Wow, what were those? They weren't normal dogs."

Lady showed up a minute later looking a tad worried, too. Wildness tinged the air. We continued on and both dogs stuck close. Emma's own fear kept her near my heels. Lady prefers roaming far and wide; this time she stayed around, no doubt out of an innate duty to protect me. Coming upon the scat of bear, bobcat, and coyote is not unusual and the dogs always sniff enthusiastically. This was our first encounter with a wild animal. After my own adrenalin quit pumping, the experience brightened my day. They are out there—the wild, the untamed, the dangerous, and unpredictable. Thankfully, the edge of wild is off limits to complacency.

Once we hit middle age and start settling in, there's a tendency to start settling for less. Unrealized dreams begin folding up, aches and pains become a commiserating theme over tea with friends. What's more, we think we can see all the way down the road as if a linear blueprint is in place: get old, stop adventures, stay put. When the author May Sarton turned fifty-four, she moved to an old farmhouse to live alone in the rural New Hampshire countryside and reported in *Plant Dreaming Deep* that life on the edge of town meant being alert to changes in the sky and to every noise.

I was forty-five when I left the studio apartment in Santa Fe to live where raccoons snitch cat food from the porch and bears steal seed from the birdfeeders. It took time for my cells to adjust, like a plant getting used to more light. Once I moved to the forest, they quickened all the more with every dip and rise in temperature, with all the yipping of coyotes. Sarton wrote that her new level of awareness shattered the sense of rest and serenity that she had expected to find in the country. Another bonus living away from town and living alone is no longer having anyone else to blame. You come face to face with yourself.

And that's not such a bad thing.

Three

Exactly 450 million years ago to the day, algae began moving out of the oceans and onto land, some adapting to fresh water and some finding sunshine and carbon dioxide to their liking. These latter became mosses and ferns. A few more million years passed and the ferns that favored sun began sprouting stems to take them a notch higher for more sunlight. These were the beginning of trees. The controversy whether trees evolved from ferns or not continues, but all you need to do is stroll through a stand of pines, squint your eyes, imagine deeply, and every tree becomes a giant fern. The shape couldn't be more identifiable.

The genus *Pinus*, the plant group that germinated the first pine trees from those tiny fern-trees, began puffing spores into the air and moving onward. This took place during the Carboniferous period 200 to 300 million years ago when land masses began breaking up. As the lands moved, the tiny pine-fern trees began finding niches that perfectly suited them. Of the ones that liked spots of low rainfall some became ponderosas. Equipped with a diverse set of genes, precisely because of the millions of years they tried out different areas, ponderosas send down roots in an amazing array of habitats—from sea level on up to 10,000 feet. These trees thrive in thick, salty air as well as thin mountain atmospheres.

I live close to 7,500 feet and even though ponderosas are well suited to areas with low rainfall, I've noticed if a seed takes root in a spot that gets a tad more runoff, it's quite happy. Maybe a bit too happy. Years ago a clump of young ponderosas grew close to my house along the east bank of a small arroyo. Periodically, during heavy rains, the arroyo fills with running water, and I'm sure the roots of those ponderosas slurped up as much as they could. I kept my eye on those trees. Providing a nice spot of summer shade, they were also what the forestry industry calls "dog-hair stands"—trees all the same age, all growing at the same pace, and all standing too close together. In fifteen years they'd be huge and overcrowded. Culling them seemed the only remedy; in doing so I got my first taste of lumberjacking and can now say with utmost authority: It's not easy toppling trees. Even small ones.

Using a hand pruner I started thinning the smaller trees. Up to three inches in diameter, they were relatively easy to guide on the way down. In fact, some I could hold with one hand while sawing with the other. Those out, next came the bigger ones. That's when I invited my friend Bonnie up for a workday. She was my co-conspirator "fucking white lady" when we put up a fence. Ever the one to take on a challenge, she pulled her car into the driveway, got out, looked around, and said, "What needs to be done?"

I'd explained over the phone that I needed someone to help guide falling trees. Now a little hesitantly I waved toward my thick patch of forest. "There it is," I said and was surprised when she didn't turn around and leave. Felling trees is intense and dangerous especially when the trees are crammed next to each other.

"Let's get to it," she said, pulling on a pair of work gloves. Every so often she helps friends repair corrals and outbuildings on the Navajo reservation. I was amazed at her ability. Over the years I've worked with lots of people, some I hope never to work with again. Bonnie and turned out to be a great work companion. When I explained the main problem was no place for the trees to fall, she looked the situation over and quickly devised a plan.

"We cut this one and let it fall through here. Next we cut that one and aim it there. Then that other one has a place to fall and . . ."

Bonnie, a weaver by trade, repairs old Navajo rugs as a profession and has a knack for eyeing unraveled edges. Logically inclined, as weavers tend to be, her mind is orderly and precise. Between the two of us, we had the first tree cut in minutes. On the way down when it got hung up on some branches, I realized we needed a rope. And Bonnie said out loud, "Let's get a rope." I love it when two minds work together with no argument, no sparring for position. We got the rope, threw it around the top branches, pulled, and the tree came tumbling down.

We cut eight trees, all about six inches or less in diameter. When we finally stopped to take a break, Bonnie began studying the smaller ponderosas. For several months she'd talked about making a Navajo loom. "Those are just the pieces I need," she said. For her help I was glad to part with the wood and she commenced to chanting a Navajo prayer of thanks as she sliced off the branches.

We moved the rest of the logs near the fence to season. When time came to cut them a year later, I played out the extension cord and brought the chainsaw to the logs. No way could I move them to my cutting area. Even dry they were dead weight. Archeologists still ponder how these early Pueblo ancestors at Chaco Canyon brought thousands of logs down from mountains without our modern tools and trucks, but I know.

I know how they got those logs down.

These people from long ago took to the chore slowly and in rhythm. They cut the trees with stone axes and chisels, focusing every muscle, every hand on the task. Cutting trees requires full attention, awareness of everything—every move, every decision, every sound. There can be no extra thoughts.

This is how those Chaco people got their beams: one log at a time. One cut at a time. No matter what tool you're using—stone ax or chainsaw—cutting wood means taking it slow. And this is how they got those logs down from the mountains.

One step at a time.

So what's the difference between "felled" and "downed"? A lot, if you're a tree. In logging jargon a "felled" tree is one that's cut down. A "downed" tree is one that's dead and goes down on its own. Then there are the "blow downs"—ones seemingly alive and healthy that topple in a big wind, like Papa South. Not long ago I asked Rodger if he'd help me "down" a tree. Once I even asked if he could "fell" a tree for me. Another time he mentioned hauling his chainsaw up the trail to "take out the tree" that "blew over" on the path to Bear Canyon. The language around here doesn't always line up with how trees get on the ground because sometimes it's easier just saying it like it is. But the logging industry created a whole new language because when it comes to lumbering, the shortest route takes the quickest words.

Culled logs are *conkies*. The person who climbs trees to the top, lopping off branches on the way down is a *high climber*. His spiked boots are *caulks* or *corks*. A *forwarder* is a machine that pushes logs forward to the truck; transporting logs is *yarding*—taking them to the yard. The *landing* is where logs land when they're dropped off the truck. And anyone who saws trees is a *sawyer*.

Oddly enough, the word with the strangest connotation is tree, and this is because of our long-time human interaction with these stately beings. And the fact that they grow everywhere.

In Sanskrit, the oldest known surviving language, the word for tree is *dāru*, meaning wood. Over tens of thousands of years as tribes migrated to new lands, somewhere along the way the D changed to T, but not always. It depended on tradition, voice inflection, and usage. Following are words for tree in six different languages:

LANGUAGE	WORD FOR TREE
Albanian	*drû*
Russian	*dérevo*
Welsh	*derw-en*
Armenian	*targal*
Swedish	*trä*
German	*tannenbaum*
Old English	*treēow*

Since trees are integral to every culture for fuel, food, and shelter, etymologists used words for trees as another way to piece together commonalities between languages. This worked well because so many of the same trees grow in so many different habitats and enviornments around the world. What people called the trees in various places provided links and clues to the source of their language. And in the end most came back to Sanskrit. Following is an example of Sanskrit and English tree names:

Sanskrit	English
bhurja	birch
wyt	willow
alysos	alder
ulmo	elm
os	ash
abul	apple
bhago	beech

Linguists also took snippets of words for common objects from around the world—like sun, moon, mother and father—and created a hypothetical system of root words and called it the Indo-European (IE) language. Nearly all languages trace back to this system of root words, which on closer inspection look amazingly close to Sanskrit.

The IE root *deru* means firm and solid (which, of course, is the quality of wood) and shows up in Latin as *dūrus*, meaning hard. Then it shows up as *drus* in early Celtic for the word *oak* and in their word *dru-wid*, which means "knower of trees" and eventually became Druid, the Celt's high priests, the ones who communed with trees for insight and guidance. Today, the branch of botany that studies trees is dendrology. The science of studying tree rings is dendrochronology.

As *deru* moved on to Old English, it became *traust* as in trust, true, truth, truce, and even betrothal. All these words derived from that innate quality of *tree*: solid and steadfast.

The other day while reading on the couch I was startled at a knock on the door. Cipio, a man who does odd jobs around my place, had brought a load of scrap wood. "I bring this before winter. I know I said I'd call first but..." and he shrugged a little apologetically, gesturing toward his small red pickup brimming with board ends from a construction job.

"No problem. Let me get my gloves and I'll help you." He wouldn't hear of it.

"It's what I can do for you." His words fell into that sing-song lilt of Hispanics still very rooted in the old ways. The soft rolling inflection comes from generations that mixed English with Spanish, or Spanglish as it's called. When I first moved to New Mexico, the sound rubbed me the wrong way like scrapings against a stone wall. To my pompous over-educated Anglo ears the accent carried the mark of illiteracy. Now things have changed. I consider hearing the undulating tone a privilege. Listening to the uplift at the end of sentences, even at the end of the shortest words is like being submerged in a warm secret language that few hear anymore. When I taught school in the small Hispanic town on the central plains of New Mexico, the old families traced their ancestors back four hundred years. When speaking English, their lilting voices rolled as easily as the wind across the vast grasslands.

I followed Cipio out to the truck and pulled back a tarp covering a woodpile. "You can see how much junk wood I have," I said, thinking it'd be a good spot to toss this new wood.

"No," he corrected and brushed my words away in that gesture so many Hispanics use, a quick flicking motion off to the side. "This isn't junk wood. I bring you good wood. *Sí?*" And he held up a chunk of thick plank.

I quickly realized that one man's scrap wood is another man's junk pile and all a matter of semantics. "Yes, it's perfect. Let's put it there," I said, and turned to lift the ax from the middle of my chopping block, leaned it against the stump, and sat down to watch. He'd brought his teenaged son along and they set to work. Sitting by and not helping made me fidgety; but I understood the etiquette. A few months before, "his woman" as Cipio calls Vira, who works at the local store, had her purse stolen from behind the checkout counter. The money she'd gathered to pay a big phone bill was gone, their phone disconnected. Vira is tough. She's raised a few kids and hard times have been plentiful. A few days after the incident I walked into the store and asked how she was doing. Her eyes flashed with wildness. "I know who did it. Everyone does. The little bastard. He needed to buy drugs." Both her hands flew up in the air in resignation. Accumulating the money again would take forever. She and Cipio work whatever jobs come along, and both are good people.

Eight years before I'd been in dire straits myself and someone in town had given me $300 to buy wood for the coming winter. "There's no need to pay it back," he said. So I gave Vira and Cipio $300 with the condition they didn't have to pay it back. In so many ways small towns take care of their own. Still, accepting charity isn't easy and this load of scrap wood came steeped with an unspoken thank you.

"...and then I go to Santa *Fé* ..." Cipio went on, telling about picking up some building supplies for his boss. His voice fell hard on the last syllable, the accent right where it belongs, on the end, how the town's name is correctly spelled in Spanish. Who are we Anglos to mess it all up? I heard a newcomer recently say "Sant-y Fay" and I worry how long northern New Mexico can hold on to its roots and not sloppy up the names of towns.

Cipio and his son continued grabbing handfuls of boards, placing some this way, others that way so the whole thing wouldn't fall over. Also, they were conscientious about keeping a narrow pathway to my cordwood. They had talked rapidly in Spanish before starting so I figured that's what they had discussed, giving me room to walk between the two woodpiles. Perfect. "It looks really good," I said.

"This wood—it's the right size to toss in the stove. Start a fire and these will keep it all day, just toss them in one at a time," Cipio said, laying down another handful.

Watching the two of them work, I wondered how much wood I've stacked over the years. Andrew dumps my split cordwood in the driveway and the stacking begins, a mindless chore, really. *Pick up two, three or four, set them down. Go get more.* Like the opposite of using a chainsaw, which seizes all your attention, the task of stacking wood requires only rhythm set to a cadence of grace. That's a little more poetic than what the job really is, yet the repetitive movement does create a trance. *Pick up two, three or four, set them down. Go get more, go get more.* Cling-bing-ting. Like the steady beat of shamanic drums the art of stacking wood sings each piece into place. Clink-clang-cling. Wood lifts to a stiff music and the slow tempo moves the logs into rows. *Go get more, go get more.*

My father often reminisced about stacking wood. "Seemed whenever I walked up to a farm house to ask for work, there was always a pile of logs that needed splitting. Sometimes I was lucky and all I needed to do was stack the wood. Stacking is the easy part," he once said. His one rule was make it neat. "People always appreciate wood that's lined up and even. One time an old woman looked over what I'd done, nodded, and went back inside for some cookies fresh out of the oven." Daddy was still alive when Ted and I set out to cut our own wood and my father laughed hearing our tale about getting our "free" load of wood. He had one comment: "Next time let someone else do the cutting. Stacking is the easy part."

When Cipio's truck was finally empty, a neat row of wood stood ready for winter. "I have more. Small logs. I bring them for you. And I will call first." He smiled a little sheepishly.

"Really, I have plenty." I knew he needed to spend time bringing in wood for his own house.

"It'll be a cold winter. Not much snow this time, but cold. You'll need wood, *qué no?*"

His weather report perked my ears. He'd grown up here and knew the signs. I asked him how he knew it would be a cold winter.

"I can feel it. There'll be lots of cold days. All in a row. You'll need wood."

After Cipio left, I eyed my wood supply. Somehow as fall gets close, wood begins arriving. Last year, Nancy, who lives next door, arrived home with a truck full of wood. Her parents had torn down their old barn.

"I couldn't bear to see all that wood go to waste so I brought as much home as I could. Do you want it?" She knew what my answer would be and even helped toss it into yet another pile. I took the offer as a gesture of truce. After she first moved here, buying the place from the family with kids, I found a note tucked on my car one morning informing me I needed to clean up the junk around my yard. This riled me no end. The piles were here first. If she didn't want to live near woodpiles, she shouldn't have bought the place. It was no different from people buying houses near airports then complaining about the planes.

I'm now glad Nancy bought the place, though. As the kids next door got older they were turning into hoodlums. The boy was especially proud that he kept getting into trouble with the police. When he dropped out of school, his parents bought him a sports car; and he thought nothing of having all-nighters when his parents were gone. So having a quiet single woman move in proved a much better situation. And not long ago she installed a woodstove to use when the electricity goes out, which isn't as often as it used to be and the durations aren't as long. Now that she's burning wood, she understands piles. In fact, she has a growing one herself. We've turned a corner into being much better neighbors.

One spring I rounded up three estimates for taking out a large ponderosa, the tree that had lost its forked branch in Rodger's yard. Several people had assured me that the ripped area where the branch broke off would pitch over and heal, that it would be stronger than ever. The tree looked suspiciously fragile the longer things went; if it fell it would crush Rodger's storage shed, an old singlewide trailer.

The first man who came by, in the middle of quoting me $1,000, looked across the canyon and noticed patches of brown on the sides of the cliff. "So the bark beetle has gotten up here, too," he said. He didn't get the job. The trees across the way weren't dead. In fact, they weren't even trees. It was early April. The brown patches were scrub oak that hadn't leafed out yet.

Another man came up with a quote of $1,500 along with a litany of ropes and pulleys and three guys climbing up to top the tree and on and on. He'd even haul the wood away for free.

I finally called Andrew, someone who knew dormant scrub oak from dead piñon trees and someone who wouldn't dare suggest taking away the wood. He came up one afternoon, looked the job over, and said he could do it for $500. Deal. He returned two days later with a helper. In a matter of minutes they'd dropped the entire upper portion of the tree over the fence into Rodger's yard, right where Andrew said it would go. It didn't even touch the fence but landed on the other side right between two small trees, not even breaking a branch on either one. They felled the rest and fifteen minutes later the trunk was sawed into short lengths along with the branch that had fallen from Nancy's tree into my yard.

When all the commotion was over, Andrew said, "You won't need wood for two years." Still, he wasn't surprised when I called later that summer putting in my order for another two cords. "Pretty soon you can open up your own woodlot."

"Oh, you know me," I said. "There's never enough."

Four

Today my whole front yard is a different configuration from what it used to be. I re-directed the dog fence to stack cordwood and kindling closer to the house. The older I get, the less enchanting it is digging my way through two feet of snow to replenish the wood rack on the porch. I got the idea for rearranging the yard when stacking wood last year. Doing this mindless work loosens thinking patterns and you can come up with all kinds of new ideas. In fact, the plan for bringing Papa South out of the forest formed one morning while stacking wood. I needed to move a woodpile to make room for a delivery later in the season. Sloan heard the musical clinking of logs and came over pulling his garden wagon.

"You won't have to make so many trips," he offered.

"Well, you're probably right, but I don't mind the trips. It's good exercise. Besides, if I put the wood in the wagon I'd have to handle it one extra time. Thanks though."

Later I got to figuring. Andrew drops off a load of wood and I begin stacking, a bit every day. In the summer I work early in the morning. Months later when there's a bite to the air, when the weather takes a turn toward fall, I begin taking wood to the porch. Soon the first wood of the season is set by the woodstove. By then I've touched each piece of wood three times. Number four is reaching for a piece to make a fire. Living with a woodstove means a life of touching wood. As pleasant as this is, you want to handle the wood as few times as possible to keep the work load down.

After Sloan left, I realized this was part of our mating dance, and I'd turned him down. We hadn't yet become lovers, but I'd felt it coming, like a warm breeze starting up the canyon. I turned and watched him pull the wagon home; the receding view was fun. What is it about watching the backside of men? How their pants hug their hips, how their bodies swagger. There he was—white beard with a silver pony-tail—pulling a little green wagon. Cute.

What first drew me in toward Sloan was the sound of his car. Long before we even considered being friends, at two in the morning I'd stir, hearing his rumbling car far down the canyon making its way home. He'd left the electronics industry years before and took a job driving a taxi in Santa Fe, working the night shift. At some point I found myself waking and waiting for the sound of his car. As it got closer and closer to our hill, relief coated my insides. When reaching the driveway, he'd gun the engine the way guys do before turning off a car. At that point all was well. I felt safe and could go back to sleep.

Watching him walk away with the wagon, I suddenly got it. Sloan was the perfect one to help lug home Papa South. When evening came, I headed over to his place. Already on the porch, he offered me a glass of wine and we talked about the weather, the new neighbors and their dog that never stopped barking. Slowly I put it to him: "I have a favor to ask, and your wagon is the key."

He hadn't seen the downed tree because when we hiked together, we took off up the mountain behind his place and went another way. He wanted to investigate before committing to this wild project of mine. We set out the next day. Just like in life, the path getting to Slow and Easy is rough and you have to watch your footing. The trail levels out for a bit then curves over a hill. When we came to the downed tree, Sloan stood and looked a long time; he walked the length of the trunk. He surveyed the steep of the incline. I held my breath, wondering what he was thinking. Finally he spoke.

"Well, I'm game. When do you want to do this?"

Five

In another time and place my father would have thrown himself to the task of helping with Papa South. He loved working outside—shirt off, sun on his back. His muscles moved under his skin like large shifting continents. Because of him I've always favored men that show a penchant for outside work and posses a handiness with tools. Yet over the years and much to my consternation I learned that just because someone is male, it doesn't automatically equate mechanical know-how, or even an innate usefulness.

There was George, a man with an artistic bent, whose idea of working with tools was activating an electric can opener for easy dinners.

There was Bobby who put up a gate that never worked right.

There was Carl who didn't even know how to use a hammer.

There was Denny, who could certainly use tools; he'd built his own house. But he'd taken a turn for any easy way out. I'd just started exploring the forest by the time we met and Denny's dog loved accompanying me. Denny, however, preferred staying behind, always saying,

"I'll split a stack of kindling while you're gone."

This became our weekend routine. Denny would show up on Saturday, I'd take his dog into the forest and come back hours later to find a pile of kindling all neatly stacked by the woodstove. How odd, though, that I never heard him hacking away at the wood. The chopping stump is in front of the house; surely the sound would carry into the forest. It did cross my mind to ask him, yet when time came to make a fire, questioning how the kindling got there seemed moot. He even gave me a hatchet for a Christmas present—so he could use it.

Then one morning I headed for the forest, leaving him to his chore. The breeze was a tad cool so I turned back for a hat. I walked in the house and there sat Denny: on the ottoman in front of the woodstove with a stack of cedar logs next to him. He was splitting them on the small chopping block I kept near the hearth for light jobs. I often wondered how bits of wood got on the couch, on the bookshelves, on the kitchen counter. When wood chips sprinkled my sewing machine I thought maybe gremlins were at work.

Now I stood, open mouthed and stunned. I finally managed to say, "There is a rule. No splitting logs in the house." Denny was retired and took retirement seriously, spending his days lying on his bed watching TV. He'd also taken up some kind of spiritual practice that helped him claim to be a human *being*, not a human *doing*.

He also kissed like a piece of cardboard. Nothing gooshy or smoochy that gets a woman's juices flowing. A friend once said she really liked a certain man, but not the way he kissed. She figured if he couldn't kiss decently, he'd be even less inventive in bed. She broke off with him before it even got to that point. Lucky her. One time in bed with Denny I checked the clock. From the time he got inspired to the moment he was done, countdown was seven minutes. Had I missed something? When we broke up, I didn't miss a thing. No, that's not true. The next time I needed to clean the stovepipe, that's when I missed Denny.

When I bought the singlewide, it had a god-awful metal fireplace, a relic from the 1970s. I replaced it with the exact model I'd had in the doublewide, but the housing through the roof didn't allow the stove enough clearance from the wall. The installer said "no problem" and commenced to rigging up a stovepipe system that required two elbows. Had I known what problems those elbows would cause, the smarter move would have been to get a new roof. Soot catches on corners. It settles in creases. Creosote builds up along seams with a stickiness that snags more soot as the smoke passes by. A stovepipe with elbows gets hopelessly clogged in no time.

After only two months of making fires in my new woodstove with the elbows in the pipe, one morning I lit a small fire and smoke immediately billowed into the house. Denny happened to be there, and in his one heroic moment climbed on the roof only to find the spark screen completely blocked with soot. Taking it off helped for a day but cleaning the pipes was the only remedy. I called a chimney sweep and watched very closely because paying someone to do this seemed a little extravagant. Next time Denny helped and between the two of us, using a box-head screwdriver, we got the pipes back together.

After Denny was gone, the next time I cleaned the pipes, for the life of me I couldn't figure out how to get them back together. So I called Sloan. He ambled over, eyed the situation, and made me nervous. Too quiet. I like to be included in someone's thinking process especially when it concerns a project of mine. Sloan doesn't operate this way, and I should have known. The previous summer hiking back down the mountain, we came through a meadow of grama grass. I marveled at the seed heads curving back into themselves like long-lashed beige eyebrows. Sloan remarked, "There's a patch outside my window and I watch them curl." We live on slow time here. So when he took forever looking at the sections of stovepipes, I bit my tongue, quit pacing, and waited.

Finally in his slow-talking way, a remnant from his rural Oklahoma upbringing, he said: "This piece goes inside this one, not the other way around." We got it back together in no time. After that, it was a one woman job, one that needed advance planning—making sure no blizzard was on the way, getting psyched up to get on the roof at the crack of dawn (so the pipes and stove are cold), and choosing a day with nothing else to do. However, I usually expect to do laundry on those days. Getting completely covered with soot takes about two hours.

Oh, how those first few fires jump after a good stovepipe cleaning. The effort and mess is worth it every time. There's nothing like a perky fire; and having freshly scraped pipes is the only way to get one if there are elbows in the pipes. Subsequently how each fire burns indicates how the air is drawing. Slow-catching fires always announce when the pipes need cleaning. From September to the end of May, they need cleaning every three months.

Six

When the summer heat presses in a little more each day, I know the yellow pine pollen will follow soon. The day before Sloan and I set out to get Papa South was the first day of an intense pollen release. Ponderosas pollinate heavily some years, other years lightly. The duration usually lasts about four days. We couldn't change the outing because I'd borrowed another wagon and needed to return it the next day.

"Don't forget a bandana for your nose and mouth," Sloan reminded as I left his porch that evening. We'd decided to leave even earlier the following day before the breezes started and met on the access road that runs between our houses at seven in the morning. Sloan's chainsaw sat on his wagon along with a number of straps. Ready, we headed out, a caravan of little green wagons into a haze of yellow mist.

Under a microscope a grain of ponderosa pollen looks like a pinto bean. Attached at both ends is a round balloon and these itty-bitty air sacks lift the speck on the slightest breeze. Sometimes the discharge is hardly noticeable. Sometimes it's a serious dusting. As Sloan and I trudged up the mountainside yellow-green pollen covered everything—rocks, oak leaves, broken twigs, the ground. The pollen was so thick that even my teeth felt coated, despite the bandana. Luckily this brand of pollen doesn't carry the allergens that juniper and piñon do. When the ponderosas release their ballooned pinto beans, maybe you'll sneeze or occasionally rub your eyes. More likely the only evidence of ponderosa pollen is clouds of yellow dust wafting on warm breezes, making air visible and mouths dry.

We arrived at Papa South after thirty minutes of trudging and pulling the wagons through the brush. "Let's start with those big branches," Sloan directed as we paced alongside the trunk. "We'll cut them into small lengths and take those down first." We set to work limbing and trimming and in no time reduced this once stately tree to a bare minimum.

Sloan threw himself to the job; and I kept taking quick glances at the precision of his hands, his actions. That innate know-how moving through his entire body was hard to ignore. Ever since the day he helped piece the stovepipes together, I've enjoyed watching him work.

How do I explain the sensuality that throbs under my skin when he lifts a chainsaw, when he rolls up his sleeves? All his actions are clean and firm, and there's never any doubt they're rooted in the masculine. No wonder women wanted to have children with him.

Sloan's tale is filled with women lying to him so they could get pregnant. One said she was pregnant so he'd marry her. The lie became evident soon enough, and soon enough she got pregnant to keep him. Another wife quit taking birth control pills and didn't tell him. A girlfriend said she'd had a hysterectomy. Another claimed sterility. For a man who never wanted to be a father, he has children he's never seen. He's also a man who believes a vasectomy removes manliness. In taking jobs that required leaving the country, a few times it was the best way to get out of the range of conniving women. Watching him put a chainsaw to this tree, I began understanding those women. If the biology of men is to spread their seed far and wide, then the biology of women is to choose the most virile man in the tribe, the one most able to survive and pass on the genes of survival. Sloan fit a category that calls to us ladies.

I felt him watching me too, sweaty and dirty as I was. His eyes traveled across my backside, up my arms. That morning, I'd started out wearing a lightweight jacket. Not long into cutting and stacking, I took it off and felt Sloan's eyes sliding slowly across my breasts as I wriggled out of the sleeves. In three more days on a hike, we'd bed down under a tree high in the mountains after years of wondering about the body of the other. We'd give ourselves to the earth, the sky, and that night again to the moon.

But for now, we had work to do.

After a good hour of hacking away on Papa South, the pile of branches was substantial. I pulled up one of the wagons. "Some of these tie-downs will reach over the logs and under the wagon," he explained. "We can tighten them as we need to on the way down." He began taking up the ropes he'd brought—all of them well worn. When I first began spending time on his porch, I noticed he too never threw anything away. Bits of wire hung from nails. Twine that he saw along the highway, stopped for, and later wound around a board dangled from a peg. Car parts, broken rakes, axe heads without handles, warped pieces of plywood, bent bicycles, and chipped flower pots cluttered his property. But clutter isn't exactly the right word. Everything was in neat piles and all accounted for.

"When I first moved here," Sloan once told me, "the people who used to live across the road, with those miserable kids, alerted the county. A man looking very official came to the door with a complaint about my junk cars. It was a complete pleasure showing him that every one of them was registered and legal." Sloan is forever rebuilding a car here, a motorcycle there. His rickety pickup looks dilapidated, but that's the one I borrow every so often. Never once has it broken down.

As Sloan handed me the tie-downs and I began uncoiling them, I was charmed. The straps he'd fashioned were clearly homemade from sections of old webbing, a nylon belt, and various other strands of material that he'd stitched together end for end. The first time I found him on his porch at his sewing machine caught me by surprise. He was mending shirts. Ever the one for self-efficiency, he had his mother teach him to sew when he was just a kid. "Thought it might come in handy someday," he said. For many years he lived in a converted school bus, traveling from oil fields to surveying jobs. Once he showed me pictures of inside the bus. The interior was all decked out with a little sink, a stove, and a refrigerator powered by a gas generator. A lovely brass bed took up a corner next to a woodstove.

"This is a pretty fancy rig for a single guy," I said, tapping my finger on a photo of the bed piled with quilts and decorated pillows.

"Thought you were running from women. Looks like you were trying to entice them."

"Well, some happened by who stayed for a bit," he admitted with one of those disarming lopsided smiles.

The generator also ran a sewing machine. Not many roughnecks leave a day on the oil fields and return to their campers to sew. Sloan taught himself to patch clothes, make bags, and stitch pillows. He even did a bit of quilting, a talent he learned from his grandmother. It wasn't all that odd that this manly neighbor sewed. Every once in a while my father gathered a bundle of shirts, sat in front of the television, and sewed on buttons.

It wasn't lost on me how much my father and Sloan shared commonalities. Seeing this helped me understand Sloan: his silences, his moods. If I venture to his place only to find him withdrawn, the cue is taken: leave, come back in a few days, maybe a week. I learned as a child to give Daddy a wide margin during his dark moods. He was quick to slap the sides of our heads if we ventured too close during what my mother called "one of his spells." Sloan ensures distance too, but with sullenness. And he uses it like a shield.

What keeps me returning between the sullen times is Sloan let me set the parameters. From the beginning our time together was up to me. A fan of Mark Twain and Robert Heinlein, Sloan holds a healthy respect for anyone who takes up the task of pushing words around. He told me: "You're the one with deadlines and commitments. You let me know when you have the time."

Today, I log in plenty of hours at the computer before crossing the road to Sloan's. The arrangement eliminates resentment. The time I have to give is time I want to give. Emotionally content within himself, Sloan doesn't need me to need him. This makes all the difference.

Flames

&

*J*UST AS THOREAU WAS THE INSPECTOR OF snowstorms, I am the witness of wind. The other evening while stepping onto the porch to take my usual inventory of the stars, I heard a faint sighing. The tips of the trees, high in their crowns, held a rustling. Quietly passing overhead, this slight breeze was fingering the very edge of a storm. Incoming weather has direction and tends to follow a pattern; by listening, by feeling you might be able to guess what it has up its sleeve. Wind, how it behaves, is the key—light and rustling, forced and thickened, puffing in and out or blasting with staccato gusts.

The most telling is how wind travels through ponderosas. The tallest trees catch the slightest movement and become the barometer of the forest. Sloan was visiting that evening when I stepped onto the porch. I called back into the house, "In four days we're getting more snow." And a storm did arrive four days later carrying six inches of very wet snow.

Live in town and weather recedes in importance. Live where the roads get so full of snow that the snowplows get stuck, the importance of weather raises the ante considerably. It only takes getting snowed in once to learn about stocking up on canned food and packages of spaghetti. You adapt to the weather wherever you live.

A friend in Los Angeles likes to say the weather there comes in a spray can: predictable and bland. Not much turbulence sweeps through southern California, but slashing rain and blowing wind do move in. When I was a kid, crowds gathered on the bluff to watch the pounding surf. The fervor electrified us. We wanted more and more, bigger and bigger waves. Those coastal onslaughts periodically ripped through and when the storms passed, the streets were littered with pieces of trees. During such a storm when I was seven, my friend Chris phoned.

"A tree fell on your father's car." Her voice rang high with triumph because she knew more than I did.

"It did not."

"Did too."

"You're a liar," I jeered. Besides, it was April Fool's Day. Did she think I was going to fall for this? The rain had kept Daddy home from the docks and he was making donuts as he always did when it stormed.

"Go and look or you'll be sorry," Chris said.

Sure enough. A pine tree about ten inches in diameter had fallen on the roof of Daddy's old 1944 Ford. Though the roof was dented none of the windows cracked. He stopped the donut production, donned his raingear, and set about sawing branches so he could roll the tree off the car. Rather than hassle with the insurance company that would no doubt up the rate if he filed a claim, he got in the back-seat of the car, laid on his back, and pushed with his feet and legs. The roof popped out good as new. Still working in the pouring rain, he quickly sawed up the trunk for firewood before the city's tree crew took it away. Finder's keepers.

One

Split wood comes in a variety of shapes. Large logs get sliced like a pie with many triangular pieces. Smaller rounds split down the middle and these are the ones to look for; each half is flat. Lay two flat sides down crosswise. Lay two more on top, flat sides down, lengthwise like a vertical herringbone pattern. Continue upward and in no time there's a brace at either end; now you stack the wood between the braces. Easy-peasy. I used to measure the finished stacks, get out my calculator, and add it all up. But I learned Andrew never cheated me.

Pick up two, three or four, set them down. Go get more. How much simpler can life get? Stacking wood methodically—this piece here, that piece there—makes things right, and I spend a good amount of time each fall considering the yard situation: which stacks to burn first and where's the best place to put this year's delivery that will be used next year? One time I called Andrew for my usual order: one cord of split piñon, one of cedar. And I told him where to put it. For the first time I wouldn't be there for the delivery. "Just dump it in the driveway," I told him.

I came home and it wasn't in the driveway. "Hey, Andrew, about that wood..."

"You had a place all raked nice and neat and that's where I put it."

"That's where I was going to stack it."

"Oh well."

And what can you say? All that wood piled in a hodgepodge,

though, was maddening. When wood is configured like that and you go to pull a log, you never know which piece balances ten more that might come tumbling down—on your hands, your feet, into your knees. Also during the winter these piles are impossible to cover with a tarp. Along the top where you can't quite reach to toss a log to hold down the edges, snow melts and trickles. The wet wood freezes. Now you have clumps of wood sticking together that need hammering to break apart. Next comes setting a few frozen pieces behind the stove for a week to thaw. These dumped piles are a mess. When I saw what Andrew had done, my nerves rankled. The following year Andrew asked for specific instructions. "I don't want to get in trouble again," he said. And I haven't missed a delivery since. For a lot of reasons. The main one is I don't want to miss our yearly chats.

Born in Jerome, Arizona and raised near Pecos, when Andrew ventured to Los Angeles as a young man, he worked for a building materials company. He eventually became a shipping supervisor but after seven years, he came back home. "I missed the clouds, the blue sky, the change of seasons, the open country. You have to lose something to realize how important it was. I didn't know I'd already had it," he told me one time. When he returned to New Mexico, he began cutting firewood. "It was something to do until I figured out what I wanted to do," he said. That was in 1975; he's been selling firewood ever since.

Because Andrew and I only see each other once a year when he delivers wood, we take the time to catch up, grumble about the government, discuss the weather, and generally pass the time of day. He'll sometimes stay an hour. He stayed even longer when grieving for a dog he'd lost. As the sun climbed higher, we gravitated to the shade under a juniper branch. I've learned from Andrew. The second year I lived in the doublewide, he brought a load of split wood and his workers quickly tossed out the logs. In no time at all a pile formed. Then it began slipping. Instinctively, I went to catch the pieces, to check them.

"Just let it go," Andrew said casually. And he was right. There is no way you can stop a pile of wood from falling. When I got a digital camera, my first photo series was of stacked wood ready to fall. Nearly everyone here has stacks of wood that tend to lean after a while, and all you can do is let them go. Wood has a way all its own. Just letting it go is lesson enough to carry into all the parts of our lives.

Two

Sloan came over this evening to sip brandy and play a game of chess, and as usual he walked in the door and asked if he could start a fire, already striding across the living room. That raw, primitive pull for making fires has hold of him too; he warms his place with a forced air furnace run by propane so a fire is entrancing. Fine by me if he wants to make a fire. When mid-March rolls around, the joy of heating with wood has worn a little thin, especially during really cold winters like this one, the one Cipio predicted.

Days and days of relenting cold and little snow mean I need to keep a fire going all day, all night. When snow accumulates on the roof it provides insulation, trapping the heat in the house. Not this year. Not enough snow. As the thermometer hovers around zero or below, tossing in logs becomes an hourly task, one I wake myself for throughout the night. If possible, you don't want ice crystals on the windows in the morning. That's really cold. During my Colorado days when I returned to school for a teaching certificate, for one week the day time temperatures dropped to minus sixty-nine degrees; that's below zero. That's really, really cold. In fact, my father called to tell me Anchorage, Alaska was eighty degrees warmer.

The San Luis Valley, where the college was, often makes weather headlines as the coldest spot in the nation. Hemmed in east and west by mountain ranges the cold settles in and doesn't lift till spring. One morning when class was underway a woman trundled in apologizing for being late. "I wanted to wash my hair, but the shampoo was frozen. Had to thaw it out in the microwave." As she laughed, the rest of us joined in, knowingly. I lived in a place where the pipes had frozen on my wing of the house and wouldn't defrost until late April. That poor professor, though. The look on his face was of total incomprehensibility. He must have thought he'd landed in a third-world country. Obviously he'd lived a life of privilege in houses that registered a steady seventy degrees on the thermostat every day all winter long.

When temperatures dip below freezing, my woodstove gets center attention around here. So sure Sloan can make a fire and keep it going all night if he wants. But he makes fires all wrong.

I build sculptures every time I assemble a fire. My method is slow, methodical—setting a split log in the ashes, tucking crumpled newspaper in front of it. Next, a handful of twigs, the ones I've gathered during the fall, get organized on top of the paper. Can't use too many. You don't want to use them up. Next comes an arrangement of junk wood, so much the heart of any new fire. Straddling wood pieces together is no different than playing with building blocks—teetering one piece across another, chunking them together. Whatever kindling happens to be in the house, whatever tinder fills the wood box near the stove determines the shape of these winter sculptures. Sometimes the designs rise prettily; other times I hold my breath that they don't topple over before I touch a match to the paper.

Sloan's method is rougher. A man's fire, I tease him. He too lays a split log in the ashes and arranges all the small and medium pieces around it. Then for a grand finale crams another log on top of the whole pile. "That way you don't have to add wood so soon," he explains. We each have our way of doing things. Still, because it's my woodstove, my house, I find myself biting my tongue. You're not supposed to do it that way, I want to cry out. But differences are nothing to fault.

After telling Sloan about an award I once earned at Girl Scout camp for making a one match fire—the only one in my unit so bestowed, I might add—that became his goal. "See, my way works too. And with one match," he boasts every time. Yup, his fires readily catch and ladder up just like they're supposed to, so I merely pour snifters of brandy and we sit before the woodstove, touching the rim of our glasses. "To another fire," we say and sit in easy quiet until one of us gets out the chess set. Then a good natured rivalry stirs as the pawns begin their march across the board. Chess becomes a prelude to other games, ones under the covers that never fail to keep us warm with burning fires of our own.

I was in second grade when I learned just how easily wood burns. A little girlfriend was coming to play at my house after school. What we'd do was all mapped out. At lunch time I unfolded a piece of paper covered with diagrams that were numbered for easy reference. They were pictures of different ways to make a fire: teepee, pyramid, lean-to, trench. I explained to Sandy how each would burn and pointed out the one we were going to make that day. The pyramid was the most dramatic. You laid a foundation of big pieces, the ends overlapping forming an open square. From there you laid more pieces, stuffing the center as you went with leaves and twigs. As you stacked more layers, bringing the box shape higher, each succeeding level was of smaller and smaller pieces. Finally a match touched through a slit near the bottom rung ignited the center rubble.

The design worked perfectly. We were in my secret fort in the backyard, a big wooden crate Daddy had brought home and reinforced with plywood. He'd placed it against the house and even fashioned a window on the south side. An old canvas tarp draped over the front. Sandy and I huddled inside, and I struck a match to my pile. Within seconds the wood exploded into flame and gathered a force I'd never seen the likes of. Fear coursed through me. Smoke filled the tiny enclosed area. The out-of-control flames blocked the entrance. They were already licking the top of the box crate. I knew the wooden eaves were overhead. Wood piles surrounded the crate. And we were trapped. The next thing I knew Daddy threw back the tarp and yelled, "What the hell are you doing?"

To this day, I'm still amazed at his timing. He wasn't due home for another two hours. That's why I thought we were safe. I knew he'd never let me make a fire outdoors without supervision. Luckily he'd come home early and wandered out back to see what he could see.

He scooped up handfuls of dirt and threw them on the fire. He scattered the sparking pieces of wood, quickly snubbing the fire. Sandy and I scrambled out and Daddy sent both of us to my room to wait until Sandy's mother came to get her. That night I couldn't watch the Mickey Mouse Club and knew the subdued talk at the dinner table was my fault. My humiliation ran deep. Yes, I could have burnt down the house. I could have seriously hurt myself and Sandy. I could have caused a lot of trouble. But I'm afraid the lesson didn't stick.

I still like playing with fire.

Three

On the wall behind my stove hangs the old branding iron Daddy picked up somewhere along the way. It hung from a hand-forged metal hook on the wall by the fireplace all my growing-up years; it might as well be with me the rest of my life.

Going through the closets and drawers after my mother's death, I came upon the blueprints for the fireplace. My parents built the house before I was born. Funny I'd never considered any planning went into making the fireplace, it just was. Studying the diagrams, I remembered my mother once said, "Your father gathered every stone from around the place when we trenched the foundation." Those chunks of sandstone became the hearth and facade on the wall over the brick chimney; all the stones were flat but deeply textured. As a child I sometimes ran my hand over them as if feeling for bumpy messages like secrets from the earth.

After finding the plans, I gazed at the stones remembering how our fireplace had become a god, an entity that kept the damp ocean air at bay.

The first fire of the season was always exciting. "I think I'll make a fire tonight," Daddy would say. Those words always marked the beginning of winter. After dinner when he and my mother finished the dishes, Daddy grabbed some of the newspapers from a pile by the door, crumpling them as he strode across the living room. He folded back the flimsy hinged screen, knelt before the fireplace, and reached for a weathered board. He was sure and competent, nimbly slicing small bits into a neat handful of kindling. He'd get the fire going, sit back on his heels, and watch the new flames climb. "Always nice to see fire again," he'd sigh—the exact words I use with the first fire every September.

We each had our designated place at the dinner table and because I was the only one who could see the fire while we ate, I had privilege. My sister and I always had to ask permission before leaving the table, except I could leave without asking when the fire needed tending. It was a job bestowed upon me by myself—stir the coals, throw on another piece of wood, keep the fire going. One time I forgot and the fire went out. Daddy remained huffy for the rest of the evening, and now I know why. Re-starting a fire means using more kindling, and kindling is always at a premium.

When I grew up homework didn't exist in elementary school. Bringing school work home was something the older kids did, the fifth graders. It was something to look forward to. So every evening after dinner Cathy and I went into the living room and sat in front of the fire to play Old Maid or Candy Land. If we didn't want to play a game or play with our dolls then gazing into the fire was good enough. We didn't get a television until I was in the third grade and with it came a rule. We could only turn it on with Daddy's permission, and we could only watch what he wanted us to. Considering how quickly television took over households, I'm grateful that our father was so stringent. Watching mindless shows didn't become a habit. I haven't had a television for twenty-five years; people wonder what I do with my time in the evenings. Not many people choose staring into a fire over watching television.

This might have something to do with where I live too. In the village nearby, I know plenty of people who don't watch television. We get together to play games. We'll play dominoes long into the night and have rousing games of cribbage. It's a different lifestyle here. Some of us don't have cell phones; some don't even have computers.

Unfortunately, I can't say that. I feel tied to mine but also feel lucky I need to keep the home fires burning. Dealing with woodpiles and splitting kindling takes me outdoors. An idea emerged the other night that the Internet is the global campfire. How many people before a screen—whether sitting down at a desk or holding a gizmo in their hand—become entranced as if watching flames? Maybe the word "obsessed" is better. The screen isn't as soothing as a fire but without stretching the metaphor too much, chumming up to a campfire for storytelling and sharing bits of our lives is not too off the mark when it comes to the Internet. Now with Skype, this new fangled Internet is even more interactive, evermore entrancing. Still, nothing takes the place of a real fire, whether in camp or in the home.

An abundance of liquid lives in fire, and fluidity opens the heart of every flame. Gaze into fire and flames become currents of water; reaching in to feel the lapping ripples is only an impulse away. Daddy used his hands to move pieces of burning wood, divide sparking sticks, reposition smoldering logs. Sometimes flames silently licked his wrists like quiet orange tongues. If a fire faltered, he'd blow steadily onto coals to start them dancing again, his lips pursed and close as if kissing hot wood.

I never understood why Fulton needed to use bellows whenever he built a fire. Even with all that excess air, the wood took forever to catch. One evening in exasperation I finally asked, "Why do you always do that?"

Crossly, and in that tone of voice that insinuates you're stupid for even asking, he said to get the fire going.

"Well, I've made a million fires and never needed one of those," I said.

His impatience snapped; he threw down the bellows, told me to do it, and headed for the kitchen for another drink. I knelt in front of the woodstove, did what needed to be done, and got the flames roaring in no time.

Kneeling before a fire is close to uttering a prayer. It's a bow to the gods of fire, of wood, of ashes, sparks, smoke, and soot. These gods hold it all, what it takes to have warmth and a sense of home. You're either drawn to the world of flames or you're not. Up before anyone else, I was the one who made the morning fires when we went camping, probably starting at age four. Before anyone scrambled out of their sleeping bags, the hearth would be warm, the griddle hot for pancakes. No one taught me how to make a fire; but the movements I'd watched were a gift, something my hands accepted easily. "Even when you were little, you'd squat by a fire stoking it with little twigs and branches. You always had such patience with fire," my mother reminisced when visiting me the winter before she died. She came to love the radiating heat of my woodstove, the ambiance of fire through the glass door. "This is so much nicer than a fireplace, isn't it?"

After Daddy died, she installed a forced air heater, shut the damper in the chimney, and finally had a warm house. When she visited me that winter, she loved watching the flames through the glass door.

The mind of the arsonist is easy to understand. Hot, blazing flames magnetize a primitive soul buried beneath our civilized ways. Fire in its destruction is complete, and the lift and thrust of wild, bursting flames release a latent craving for power. When I taught school in that small plains town, every year before the big football game with our rival school a bonfire fueled the team with adrenalin. Somewhere back in our Neanderthal minds, the vicious enthrall of hot, hot heat still lives. When so much of the West burned in the early part of the new millennium, some of those fires were deliberately set, adding to the rising chaos. During the madness of the fire that burst through Los Alamos taking out four hundred homes, two young men set fires at both ends of the box canyon where I live. We were told to evacuate. Sloan didn't, I did. Driving away with a few meager belongings (and were they the right ones?), I thought about the boys who'd set the flames. So entranced with fire they wanted more, more! That manic madman craving huge, hot, unbridled ruin had consumed them. People obsessed with fire need to live with a fireplace or woodstove so the fascination can transform into yielding heat.

Watching fire through glass doors is like staring into a great crystal ball: a trance envelopes you. People wonder if I ever miss the ocean. No, living in the mountains makes up for it. Besides, whenever I light a fire, the water is there in all its swelling and ebbing tides. It'd be even better if painted wood exploded into colors again. In bygone days some of the boards Daddy brought home from the docks were finished with lead-based paint. No one worried about that then and the burning paint turned into green, turquoise, and blue flames—all the colors of a deep burning ocean. Even without the ocean's hues, soothing flames lap against the glass doors like waves rubbing against pilings.

The spirit of water lives in fire. Some mornings I'm late getting started because before dawn when darkness encircles the house, a fire rolling with heat calls me in and won't let go.

Four

Who knows what the coyotes were up to this morning. For nearly an hour they barked that quivering, chittering, yap-yap-yipping. Needing more kindling, I waited until all was quiet. No need to run into a pack if you don't need to. Finally I set out, dogs at my heels, and brought back a bundle of damp twigs. I set it near the hearth to dry, and Emma ignored the twigs. As a puppy, she devised a game of grab-bing one end of a branch then pulling and tugging until the whole kit-and-caboodle came loose on the carpet. She loved wrangling twigs, and I let her. Watching how her mind worked was fun. Equipped with three sets of herding genes, one time she nosed a bunch of loose twigs into a pile, crouched at them, and barked. This was right after she had discovered barking. After she discovered leaping, she snatched a twig and commenced to leaping from one end of the living room to another. Now she is content to take up a rawhide chew and go to work.

I knelt before the woodstove and just as I opened the door, a siz-zling red coal popped out and landed on the carpet. Immediately I flicked it onto the hearth. If ashes are the downside of heating with wood, sparks are even worse. They've landed in my hair, flown in my face, singed my hands, burnt holes in my clothes. And it doesn't take long, right after getting new carpet, for a hefty ember to zing out and leave a black gouge. Dry wood can contain trapped air; when heated, the air pops, spewing pieces of glittery burning wood. The best spark happened one evening when I was ten years old.

The fireplace blazed while my family watched television. I was ly-ing on the couch. Suddenly everything happened at once. A woman in the show started screaming at the same time a huge cinder—I saw it out of the corner of my eye, orange and glowing—flew over the fireplace screen. The thing missiled right toward me, landing on my neck. I started screaming. My father reached over from his chair and whacked me on side of my head. "For Christ's sake, I can't hear the god damned television!"

My mother and sister screamed at me to quit screaming. Clearly, I was upstaging the woman on TV. And I wouldn't stop. I was writhing on the couch, my hand clutched my neck. My sister finally came over and pulled my hand away, now also burned. "You're really hurt!"

When the dust settled, everyone said they thought I'd been trying to out-scream the woman on T.V. For years I had a slight mark on my neck from that night.

You have to be quick with sparks, especially during molten sprayings. These are like fireworks in July, only they're in your house. I used to keep a throw rug by the stove, but kept tripping over it. I kept a wooden scraper at the ready, but a housesitter threw it in a fire and burned it. Now I just squelch sparks with the blunt end of a hatchet. My father never kept anything around to deal with sparks either. They are part of the unpredictable nature of fire.

When choosing what to bring back after my mother died, there was no question about the old copper washtub. Long after I'd left home, Daddy found the tub at a flea market; it was perfect for holding kindling. He told me about dickering for it with an old man "...and we got to talking...he used to work a goldmine up in Fallon, Nevada right in the area where I did." The man's wife had left him for the bright lights of Las Vegas and he headed for the dry, hardscrabble hinterlands of the desert. He built a shack of boards, tires, and old license plates, turning himself into a contented desert rat. Anyone who thumbed their nose at society got a thumbs-up from my father. "He let me have the tub for only a few dollars."

Tucked in a file in a drawer of my parents' papers, I found the deed to that goldmine in Fallon. I called the county clerk to ask about its history and was told "...those old mines needed to be worked every year in order to keep the deed." Sixty years or more had passed since my father's stint at being a desert rat. I kept the deed out of sentimentality, and one night mentioned it to Sloan. Lo and behold even he had done some prospecting near Fallon.

"I was living in the Sierras and partnered up with another man. Didn't cost much and we had ourselves a goldmine," he said. "The place had been mined clean by then, but we got it for cheap. The deal was we'd split everything fifty-fifty at the end of the summer. We each cashed in a few nuggets, or so I thought. A few days later his wife showed up with a new car. He'd pocketed more rocks than I even guessed was there."

When much of Papa South was sawed up, Sloan hefted the trunks onto the wagons. I arranged sections of large branches on top. We lashed them down tight. The loads were heavy and by the time we started down the mountainside we were both sweaty with smears of yellow-green pollen on our cheeks, foreheads, and arms. We went in relays, deploying one wagon part way down; we tucked rocks under the tires to keep the wheels from rolling then hiked back for the other wagon. Sloan tied ropes to the back of each so he could hold the tension and not let the wagon slam into the backs of my legs as I held the tongue and guided it down the path.

The route wound circuitously through the trees to avoid the rocky arroyos. If a wagon wheel got hung up on a rock, there'd be trouble. No way could we back up and go around. Gravity made sure of that. The load necessitated a downhill direction all the way.

It reminded me of pioneers routing the big Conestoga wagons across rivers. Some accounts of these crossings report days of ferrying a hundred or more wagons. Men died, children drowned, horses, and wagons were swept away. Sloan and I didn't lose any personnel; still, the ordeal was arduous.

I'd measured Papa South after he'd gone down. The girth came in with a seventy-inch circumference; the diameter was twenty-two inches. Not a small tree. Not an easy day.

The sun blazed, making the pine needles crackle under each step. We tussled with the wagons for a nearly an hour before finally reaching my yard where we unlatched the ropes and rolled off the logs. Both of us stood, hands on our hips catching our breath. And this was just the first haul. We wordlessly looked at the jumbled logs—the landing, they say in logging camps—and I felt some measure of satisfaction. The plan had worked. We went back for another load.

In his younger days Sloan hired on with companies that took him to the Aleutian Islands, Iran, Germany, and he never tires of telling about working three winter seasons with a rowdy crew on the North Slope of Alaska. On a dusty shelf in his house he has photo albums filled with pictures from a life working with heavy machinery. From backhoes to front loaders and bulldozers he began working with monstrous equipment when he was only eighteen after taking a job clearing roads with the Forest Service.

Who else could have helped take out Papa South? Bonnie would have been willing, but I needed someone with more strength. That usually means a man. Asking Rodger was out of the question. He'd want half the take, and I didn't want any sharecropping with this. This tree was mine. So it just made sense that this neighbor, a man right across the way, a man who knew the machinations of bringing down a tree was perfect for the job.

We coordinated easily, bringing down that tree. After Papa South was finally in my yard, there was little to keep us apart now. How a man and woman work together so often mimics lying in bed and anticipating the needs of the other. We found a rhythm in work that let us enter the heat of coming together, welcoming the sparks as they arced between us. The slow burn finally got ignited.

"I think we could have made it easier on ourselves," Sloan says now when we talk about bringing down that tree. Frequently the event swings back into view like turning a favorite crystal in the sunlight. His mind ever forging another project, not long ago he said, "I want to make some sides for the wagon. That way the logs would be less likely to fall off. Yeah, that'd be the better way to go."

As if we're going to do this again. But you never know. Trees fall all the time out here.

Several years before, I became obsessed with measuring trees, diameters and circumferences. I'd been reading about David Douglas, the explorer from Scotland responsible for naming the Douglas fir and the ponderosa. He measured trees in the Northwest Territory during the early 1820s, some coming in at *fifty-seven feet* in circumference. That's the distance around the tree! Huge. I notched my walking stick in twelve-inch increments and began a bout of measuring. For my life, though, I couldn't remember how to find the diameter of a circle. Googling tree farms and the Forest Service would surely turn up the formula. Not so.

The commonly accepted measurement with the tree industry is "dbh" or "diameter at breast height," which is four-and-a-half feet above ground. Fine. But how do you get the diameter without knowing the diameter? And what happens if your tree isn't four feet high? Googling "equation for diameter" didn't help. I got pages of math sites, but you needed to know the diameter to find the diameter.

$$\text{CIRCUMFERENCE} \div \text{DIAMETER} = \pi$$
$$\text{CIRCUMFERENCE} = \pi \times \text{DIAMETER}$$

I did remember that π or pi, was a set number with a value of 3.1415926535897, or 3.14 for short. I remembered equations could be rearranged if you knew what you were doing. Math is just beyond me. I called Sloan. Some of the first computers he worked on were the size of large rooms. One time stationed on an island that faced Russia during the Cold War, he kept part of the United States defense system from falling apart. By the time we met he was studying commodities and had created all sorts of intricate number crunching programs. I figured if anyone could find the diameter, he could.

The next day he phoned. "It works with coffee cans and plates. It should work with trees," he announced. He'd turned the formula around and came up with this:

$$\text{DIAMETER} = \text{CIRCUMFERENCE} \div \pi$$

Simple. Trying it with stumps in my yard, I measured around the outside and across the top to double-check. The formula worked every time. I threw on my hiking gear and hurried to the mountain for a day of measuring. I later learned that "dbh" came from surveyors working in snow country. Chances are if they marked a tree at breast height, they might be able to find it during heavy snows.

Listening to my measuring forays a few days later, Sloan presented his own idea. "If you ever come across any breasts four feet off the ground, I'm the one who gets to measure them."

Deal.

Five

The other day Sloan and I met up with Rodger and Julie on the mountainside. Snow had fallen the day before and all of us were following animal tracks. During the summer, you'd think the forest was devoid of any living creatures. Only the occasional droppings of scat let us know animals really do frequent the place. However, after the slightest snow, an entire menagerie of prints shows up—lions, bobcats, turkeys, deer, elk, mice, voles, skunks, squirrels. Coming upon raccoon prints is fun; they really do have miniature hands. Even a wolf has moved in. I heard it once. The howl raised my hackles. Rodger listened to a distant moaning once, too, not dog or coyote and finally determined it was the wolf. In the snow its paw prints measure huge enough to make the tracks of Julie and Rodger's two big Rottweilers seem trifling.

As we stopped on the trail, Sloan told them another item we'd come across the day before. "We followed what looked like a person dragging something. Turned out they'd cut a fairly decent sized Douglas fir, leaving a three-foot stump. Then they topped it, taking about four feet for the perfect Christmas tree."

A lot of footprints surrounded the poached tree so several people had been involved. The cross-section displayed about fifty rings, which meant that once upon a time a little seed found a warm moist place to settle down, sprout a taproot, and take hold. It had reached a height of thirty feet before someone decided they wanted a nice tree for Christmas.

"They killed a tree so they could have part of it in their house for five days," Sloan said. One of the reasons he chose to become a hermit was to remove himself from the general stupidity of the human race.

"Well, this is my favorite Christmas tree," Julie said, lightening the mood and walking a few feet up the trail, "and I'm going to keep it right here." She touched a young Douglas fir, about five feet high. Over the years I'd also watched this little guy. It was just a smidgen, a six-inch seedling when I first came across it. Out in the open and away from competing trees, it gets all the sunshine it needs so the north side isn't stunted and misshapen. Rooted in terrain slightly wrinkled in a spot that catches run-off, it is a very happy tree.

"Next year let's decorate it," Julie suggested. "We can bring up all kinds of ornaments." That primal urge to hang ornaments in trees runs strong. In my favorite spot on the mountain is another fir tree, one only a few inches high when I found it. Over the years I've hung rocks and feathers on its branches, leaving it adorned year round. Decorating live trees reaches back thousands of years, no matter what part of the world. The Druids tied apples to limbs to thank their god Odin. The Chinese strung red banners through branches. The Greeks draped special trees with garlands of flowers and dangled little masks called "oscillas" that twirled in the wind. Someone once told me the Celts also hung entrails of freshly killed deer from branches as a way to thank the gods for helping them through another winter. Humans have always lived alongside trees; our connection to them is embedded.

I was completely disheartened when Daddy told me Christmas trees came from tree farms. I was eight. That these trees weren't from a real forest put a damper on the whole show. Same thing when he said the fish we caught in the lake on our annual camping trips weren't wild either.

"The fish are raised in a hatchery," he informed me one night at the dinner table, casually reaching for the mashed potatoes. I was crestfallen. In my mind those fish needed to be wild. Our Christmas tree needed to be wild too. In school we'd been studying how things were manufactured, all in preparation for a field trip to an orange juice factory. What formed in my mind was an image of trees and fish sliding down conveyor belts. It wasn't so far off the mark. During my senior year in high school my parents dragged me and my sister on a day trip to a Christmas tree farm near the little town of Julian in the mountains behind San Diego. The day was foggy, cold, and dismal, a typical winter day along the California coast.

When we arrived at the farm my sister and I quickly ditched our parents and roamed among the trees. I felt cheated. The sign read "Pick-Your-Own from a Forest of Trees." This wasn't a forest. Straight, narrow pathways ran between rows and rows of trees. Some were tiny seedlings, others saplings, some older. No matter what section, all the trees were the same height, the same shape, the same same. Talk about dog-hair stands. This was as close to a factory as you could get.

Recently I visited a man up the road from me who runs a small scale tree farm of landscape conifers. "The tips of the leader and the lateral branches are snipped," he explained. "This clipping lets the trees bush up a bit and it sorta helps them out." I bit my tongue. Do trees really need help growing? Do they need to be perfectly symmetrical? Perhaps our conditioning to Disneyland cleanliness and McDonald's conformity makes us think so. The Japanese trim their trees in the opposite direction, letting branches reach out in divergent arcs. This asymmetry is restful and pleasing.

In an article by pen pal Bernd Heinrich, he maintains that the perfect Christmas tree resides only in our minds. He says all the clipping and snipping on tree farms has made us forget what an authentic evergreen looks like. A commercial Christmas tree starts like any other conifer, then comes the calculated trimming. Heinrich says the evergreen tree is now tamed into a bush with hardly any semblance of wildness. Maybe that's why when my family went to Christmas tree lots, we tended to always bring home a lopsided fir. A roped off area held the trees that didn't quite meet the standards. Even with all that snipping down on the farm they refused to behave. These discounted seconds always appealed to Daddy. But back at the house he, too, set about sawing off lower branches, drilling holes further up, and inserting the sawed branches. "There, the perfect tree," he'd say. They always looked nice, his modified renditions—rounded out and conical—just the way they were supposed to look. Just like those holiday trees that grow in our minds.

Conically shaped trees grow branches in tapered tiers for practical purposes. The wider, lower branches hold the snow that slips from each higher branch; their flexibility makes them adaptable to heavy snow. Rarely do I find broken branches from firs. Ponderosas, on the other hand, don't give as well in the wind or snow. Many have cracked and dangling limbs. A few are so brittle they lose branches after every major weather event.

One forty-foot ponderosa out here has only a few tufts of needles on the upper branches. Scraggily and twisted, how it manages to stay afloat is beyond me. Even the slightest wind piles more boughs around its feet. I've named this one Stick Man.

The subtle elevation changes on the mountain have all the differing vegetation hovering along the edges of transition zones. Everything tends to intersperse. Even a small grove of aspen grows in a narrow enclave in Bear Canyon; they usually like the higher elevations. At home among the ponderosas, the piñons eventually give way to the Douglas firs that are more at home in the higher reaches. On the north side of one canyon, where the last of the snow doesn't melt until late May, a dense stand of fir forms a canopy over a wide animal trail.

The first time I spotted this place with all the shade and moisture, the profusion of moss on rocks and logs, I instantly named it Fairy Moss Hill. The presence of all these Douglas firs, however, does bring some foreboding. It means a forest hasn't burned in a long time. These trees like sun—open areas that have been shaved off by floods, landslides, and fire. When they are overcrowded like Fairy Moss Hill, and dying off because they can't get the sun, it means the area is begging for fire.

The Douglas fir comes in second behind the Scotch pine as America's favorite tree at Christmas, and the fir is the earth's third tallest tree. Oddly enough they aren't real firs. The scientific name *Pseudotsuga* is a blending of Greek and Japanese for false hemlock. In 1790, Archibald Menzies, a naturalist and physician from a Scottish family of botanists and gardeners, signed on with Captain George Vancouver. Menzies traveled the Northwest Territory keeping a daily log as he tended to illnesses, but he also took cuttings of flowers, grasses, and trees. One tree was a peculiar hemlock that later became *Pseudotsuga menziesii*, named after him.

Thirty-three years later David Douglas explored the same region. Selected by the Royal Horticulture Society in 1825, this twenty-three-year-old upstart traveled with the Hudson Bay Company to explore the western part of America opened up by Lewis and Clark. During his three years Douglas logged in 2,000 miles. He shipped back cuttings and seeds, and declared this stately prolific tree would be good for lumber. Nearly two hundred years later, his prophecy still holds true. The Douglas fir is still the preferred tree for construction. Hence all the fuss over the Spotted Owls that also favor this tree.

A man who ate plants and lichen he couldn't identify, pulled tricks on the Indians, and forced his party onward into winter despite inadequate food and clothing, Douglas also did the unthinkable. Usual etiquette in botanical circles is to let someone else name a plant after you. Not one to wait for the slow scholarly wheels to turn, when Douglas came upon this fir, he gave it the common name—after himself.

My sister and I meandered through the foggy tree farm the day we went for our Christmas tree, becoming impatient with our father who was now talking with the salesman about splitting hickory logs in Michigan. Our mother was restless too. There was no forest magic here—that delightful chaos of fallen branches, downed trees, and patches of grass. Finally, the tree my father chose was sliced from its roots, flung on top of our car, lashed down, and we were off.

Pick-Your-Own tree farms exist because our culture still clings to the romantic idea of cutting a Christmas tree in a forest. It's such a Norwegian fantasy. The first Christmas Ted and I were together, we decided to spend Christmas with my parents. I wanted to bring them a real tree from a real forest.

Getting the permit was easy and the day we started our trip, we first went into the forest and cut a pretty fir. We lobbed it in the back of the truck and crossed several state lines until we pulled up along the curb in front of my parents' house. When Daddy heard what we'd done, he gamely hauled that fresh cut forest tree out of the truck like this was a real prize, which of course it was.

He quickly secured the tree in a metal stand, filled it with water, and didn't even rearrange any of the branches. In his element of having something outside the ordinary, he wanted to know all about the tree-cutting—where we went, why we chose this tree from all the others. My father's usual thirst for all the details.

Christmas tree farms make up nearly a million acres in the United States; they sell more than 30 million trees each year. The average age for harvested trees is seven years. For myself, if I want to see a Christmas tree on Christmas morning, I step out my door where none of the trees are pruned. Sometimes they're even flocked.

Six

This morning I made a fire, sat back on my heels, and watched the flames take hold. All the wood from Papa South is gone now. Years have passed since the great scavenging project, but I still remember my first fire with that wood—and how it didn't quite go as planned.

I was flying back from Oregon and realized I'd neglected to bring in wood before leaving on my trip to visit friends. After a long day of airports and tight leg room, I actually looked forward to lugging in logs. As the plane headed for Albuquerque, I knew exactly which pile to use. Papa South.

The moment had come.

Now, did I change out of my traveling clothes to bring in wood? Nope. Nearly every piece of clothing I own is smudged with soot or pricked with splinters. Even my father split kindling wearing a suit once. We'd returned from a Christmas pageant at the church, the house was cold, and first thing he did was head for the fireplace. Getting the house warm took precedence over keeping clothes neat, and still does. Even before taking the suitcase out of the car, I carried in an armful of logs and remembered how grueling it was bringing this tree down. Sloan and I made three treks that day. After grappling each load down the mountainside, we dumped the logs helter-skelter. By the end of the day my yard was a jumble of tree parts and stayed that way for several years. I wondered how I'd get it split.

Then magic happened.

New Mexico isn't called the Land of Enchantment for nothing. Serendipity wings through events like a loose spirit here. By chance the editor of a magazine I write for asked me to take the oral history of the first executive director of the New Mexico Rural Electric Coop. Carl was eighty-six and we spent hours together sitting in front of microphones recording his story. Born in Mississippi and raised in a house without running water or electricity, his slow talking Southern drawl dipped into memories long ago of the rural South. His mother cooked on a cast iron stove—winter and summer—and Carl's job as far back as he could remember was to keep the box by the stove full of split wood.

As Carl and I got to know each other, he learned I heated with a woodstove and had a yard full of logs. He insisted on bringing up his wood splitter. "You have to get that wood in before winter," he stated firmly. Two days later he showed up and with Sloan's help we began sawing logs, lifting stumps onto the splitter, then one of us pushed the lever that slowly forced a steel wedge into the stump. The wood creaked as the wedge entered the grain. With a satisfying crack the wood broke apart.

By the time we finished, a wondrous pyramid of wood, all aglow with that yellow sheen of newly split wood, stood in the driveway. Problem was it never got stacked. So once again there I was with one of those miserable piles of wood. Even so, never has there been a heap of wood that made me more proud.

For two years I had imagined burning Papa South, imagined the infused tenderness while making that first fire. I knelt before the woodstove, got the fire going, and was caught up short. I had expected to be swept into ceremony, into some sort of swooning rite of passage when first burning this wood. I envisioned lighting a fire of thanks to the forest, a ritual of warming the hearth.

Instead, I felt terrible. I was ashamed. I should have left well enough alone. Downed trees go down for a reason.

The winter following the feat of bringing Papa South home, I came upon *The Hidden Forest* by Jon R. Luoma. The book kept me engaged for months, my pace measuring only a few pages at a time. I needed to absorb the information slowly; and the night I learned downed trees are more alive than living ones, I had to step out on the porch for a breath of fresh air.

In a tree that's upright and thriving, only five percent is composed of living cells; the rest is dead wood. In a tree that's down and rotting, twenty percent is living tissue—the tissue of termites, fungi, beetles, and mites that bore into the bark and lay eggs, in turn their larvae chew the wood to pulp. These are the creatures that perform the art of returning nutrients to the earth. The tree that hosts these creatures is called a "nurse log" because it nourishes everything living on it. In wet, moist climes nurse logs also supply a "rooting media" for conifer seedlings, providing shade, water, disease protection, nutrients, and sunlight. While growing on nurse logs, these tiny trees also contribute to the breakdown of lignin, an integral part of cell walls in plants.

Up until the early 1970s the value of rotting logs wasn't even considered. In its clear-cutting campaigns, the Forest Service mandated hauling away slash. All of it. Even the small stuff got scooped up for particle board. But leave a tree on the ground and the moisture that accumulates underneath, even in arid areas, provides damp quarters for spiders, wrigglers, and all kinds of microbes.

In taking Papa South out I had defeated millions of life cycles. I'd robbed the forest of enriched soil. All the chewing that churns wood into minerals, I'd effectively stopped. In taking Papa South out, I deprived billions of little beings of a place to call home.

Years before while hiking in the higher elevations on a northern slope, I'd come upon a downed tree leisurely melting back to the earth. Judging by the surrounding trees, it was a good-sized Douglas fir. Ferns, moss, and funny shaped mushrooms sprouted from this log like fuzzy, wild vegetable hair on a rag-tag shaman. I returned to this downed tree often. Each season it shrank a bit more as the cylindrical sides sagged. Each season the entire length settled as if scrunching into an easy chair. One day after a long soaking rain I hiked to this log. All the things growing on it glistened, and I gently pinched a thick edge of broken bark. Water squeezed out, dripping a cold stream down my wrist. The wood was like a sponge. I named this tree Squishy Sue and later realized what this soggy downed tree was. A nurse log.

If I'd left Papa South alone, he too would have wilted back to the earth and become a nurse log. A lot can be said for accepting things as they are. Pieces of softness can grow under the toughest skin. Even I keep finding ways to make myself more available and not expect so much from others, especially if I'm not giving either. I am settling into a better earth myself.

I watched the flames rise as this wood I'd worked so hard for went up in smoke. My insides constricted. They didn't expand with gratitude. That was the first fire in my life that didn't bring a measure of comfort.

Seven

Funny how we look back on different phases of our lives and in quiet moments still feel the auras they hold. The nostalgia for my double-wide resides in cryptic, selected scenes: gathering driftwood, buying a chainsaw, making pies from apples picked outside my door. That past also becomes a vortex, a time that not only spit me out but spun me in, into a phase of making better decisions.

If nothing else, I've learned to pay attention to the things that don't sit well—like I didn't one morning at Fulton's after breakfast. I suggested going down to see the river. He waved me away saying he'd seen it, as if a river is ever the same.

Set this next to my suggestion to Sloan the other day that we hike to Tiny Spring, a place where clear, clean water seeps from under a log. The fresh water spreads into a shallow sandy pool then trickles downhill, forming a small ribbon of a stream that slides over mossy rocks. During the winter it freezes into a pond that Lady and Emma love rolling and sliding on. During the summer, picnicking under the tall willow trees makes a fun outing. After suggesting the hike, I remembered Sloan had taken friends there only a few days before.

"Maybe you'd rather go someplace else since you were just there."

"There's always something new to see," he said, gladly joining me in poking around the muddy edges of this amazing waterhole. Over the years we've found marks of bears, deer, and innumerable prints that birds sketch along the edges. All the creatures of the forest know how to find this water. Even us.

Though Sloan and I are more compatible, in private moments of wistfulness a thin sadness creeps in. This is what Fulton and I wanted, living together separately; and he told his friends about our arrangement as if we were embarking on the cutting edge of something new. And we were. Only both of us forgot to mention how we wanted the arrangement to be. If we'd spoken up, we might have bypassed all the years that angrily yanked us around.

Then if only I'd listened to the words of a child.

Before moving to Pecos, I went to breakfast with a friend and her ten-year-old son. Listening to our conversation he looked a little perplexed so I told him about moving a doublewide to the back of my boyfriend's property. Innocently he asked, "Why would you do that?"

And this remains the best question I never tried to answer.

A Slow Burn

*W*HEN STRIKING MATCHES THESE days, I know they aren't what they used to be; the quality is going down hill. Sulfur matches were invented in 1827. Surely, they should be getting better, not worse. Sometimes the head breaks off and flies across the room, often lit. More times than not, they don't even light. Do manufacturers think we won't notice?

Then there's a brief moment after touching a match to crumpled paper when nothing happens. That stillness before the storm. You wait. You wonder if anything will catch. You wonder if the local newspaper has again changed the quality of newsprint that only smolders and won't burn. So you wait some more and finally tiny flames find their way through air. Suddenly, poof, long strands of orange dance upward, the crackling of dry wood begins and another fire is on the way.

A few weeks ago I borrowed a log splitter from a friend, hauled it up to my place and set to work. Sloan was sick so I took on the task without him. A lot of work but doable alone. How I wish Carl could have joined me. A year after he helped split those logs, cancer took him. I got to the hospital hours before he died and didn't know what to say. This once vital man was sinking away. Finally I bent over and said, "Hey, Carl, you need to split some kindling and fill that box by the cook stove." His eyes opened, a faint smile tugged at this mouth before he dropped back into the dreamland of the dying.

When I first came around the bend and saw Papa South down, admittedly I wasn't any better than a short-sighted, clear-cutting logger. Taking Papa South out of the forest, out of the cycle of decomposing was an ecological faux pas, but I've learned; and my relation with the entire forest has changed. The trees on the mountainside are probably safe now from my scavenging ways mostly because wrangling logs is best left for younger women. On the other hand this one tree provided a lot of wood. As Andrew said when delivering cordwood and seeing all the logs, "You'll have plenty of wood for a few years." Once again he was right, though the regret would be missing our yearly chat.

I lament that my father never met Andrew. I can see them now, leaning against a pickup, talking about the weather. Surely my father would have wanted to see Andrew's woodlot, even test out that handy wood splitter. Daddy also would have enjoyed meeting Cipio, who called the other day to make sure I'd be there when he dropped off another load of scrap wood, his thick Hispanic cadence singing over the phone: "You're keeping fires day and night now, *qué no?*"

Yes, in the heart of the cold season the woodstove stays happily warm all the time. At night after I throw in an unsplit log, embers eat shallow caves into the pitch of wood, like golden termites slowly devouring roasted morsels. Burning goes on without flames and sometimes in the morning cinders wink and squint with orange glowing eyes.

Yesterday after returning from a short stint of snowshoeing I needed to bring in more wood and slipped into my Detroit coat. The cuffs are getting worn, the collar a bit frayed, and a snap broke last winter. Luckily, Sloan knows how to fix things like that and even added a few more snaps down the front. Still, I find myself parceling out the times I wear it, trying to save it from the rag heap.

This evening snow began falling, piling into thick mounds, quiet and white. Sloan came over for a big mug of hot chocolate along with a slice of my famous apple pie. After we finished a ruthless game of chess, I threw another log on the fire because during the winter burning wood is a love affair that lasts all night.

Acknowledgements

A book undergoes numerous drafts. Many thanks to those who read with insightful eyes, and often several times—Emily Drabanski, Gussie Fauntleroy, Linda Hasselstrom, Anne Hillerman, Rebecca Smith, Anna Tanaglia, and Peggy Warren.

About the Author

Cindy Bellinger lives in northern New Mexico where she grows her own vegetables and continues gathering wood. This is her fifth book with several more in the works. As for entering even more heat, she is now welding metal sculptures for her garden.

The Young Adult novel she was writing, *Wild Honey,* that caused the breakup with Fulton is now available as an ebook. Also *Into the Heat* is an ebook. Visit *www.cindybellinger.com* and view the video about the making of this book.

CPSIA information can be obtained at www.ICGtesting.com
Printed in the USA
LVOW120922291211

261379LV00003B/2/P